99 DAYS

of

WISDOM, COURAGE

STRENGTH

TRUST

FAITH

HOPE & LOVE

That Will Change Your Life Forever

DAVID MASSIE

ILLUMIFY
MEDIA.COM

99 Days Devotional
Copyright © 2025 by David Massie

The views and opinions expressed in this book are those
of the author and do not necessarily reflect the official policy
or position of Illumify Media Global.

Published by
Illumify Media Global
www.IllumifyMedia.com
"Let's bring your book to life!"

Library of Congress Control Number: 2025909753

Paperback ISBN: 978-1-964251-70-7

Cover design by Debbie Lewis

Printed in the United States of America

*This book is dedicated to my wife, who is the love of my life,
a blessed treasure, my partner in faith and ministry
and so often my inspiration, my rock, my iron,
my plumb line of faith. And to my son and his wife,
whom I adore and cherish as precious gifts from God.*

Table of Contents

Preface

THE INSPIRATION FOR this book came from the sharing of devotions through different ministry opportunities. Many friends, relatives, co-workers, and co-servants in the Lord encouraged me to put a set of devotions into book form. So here it is, and it is my prayer you are greatly blessed reading the book.

The title is rather bold in that it declares by you reading these devotions your life will be changed forever. I firmly believe this to be true if you earnestly and sincerely set your heart as you to meditate on the devotions. Read with diligence, praying before reading that God would open your heart to receive blessings of wisdom, courage, strength, trust, faith, hope, and love He has in store for you. Read with an openness, an expectancy, and commit to sharing your thoughts and prayers, and your life will be changed forever. It is a promise from God.

> *"So my word that comes from my mouth will not return*
> *to me empty, but it will accomplish what I please*
> *and I will prosper in what I send it to do."*
>
> —Isaiah 55:11 (CSB)

To those who do not know the Lord Jesus Christ, I pray this book finds you ready to enter into the promise of eternal life. We all come into this world as sinners, but God gave us His son to pay the penalty for our sins. It is in Christ, and Christ alone sins are forgiven before God. He is the way, and the truth, and the life. No one comes to the Father except through Him (John 14:6).

God proved His love for you and me and all in that while we were still sinners, Christ willingly died for us (Rom. 5:8). The night I gave my heart to the Lord, I responded to this same message and invitation, reasoning in my mind that if what the preacher said was true, then I wanted to know more. I went forward and received salvation through the grace of God and my life was forever changed.

—Pastor David Massie

Daily Devotions

DAY 1

"And we know all things work together for good to them that love God, to them who are the called according to His purpose"

—Romans 8:28 (KJV)

WHEN WE ARE in a time of crisis or pain or isolation it tests our faith. Do we truly believe and take to heart the Words of the Bible? Do we truly trust that God is working for good in this pandemic? Are we truly overcoming our fears with faith?

As a new pastor called to the East Coast it was a just a few months into the ministry when the 9/11 attack occurred. I vividly remember within a week I was taking ministry trips into New York. Never forgetting the city that never sleeps. Walking along empty, dusty, Manhattan streets to about a half block from ground zero. The area was devastated and looked like a war zone. Subsequent trips revealed an eerie silence among the people who had a look of shock on their faces as they walked around the city. But the most heart-wrenching recollections were the memorials in front of the fire stations across Manhattan. Along the sidewalk were flowers piled two, three, and sometimes four feet high. And there were pictures of the fallen posted on the fronts of the stations. These were husbands, and fathers, sons, and brothers. The tears of the passersby's caused emotions to well up inside of me, and I could not help but ask Why God? Where is the good in this?

Questions we are not alone in asking. In this life there will always be times that test our faith. Moses asked, "Lord, why have you brought trouble on this people?" (Exod. 5:22 NIV). Gideon asked, "Why has all this happened to us?" (Judg. 6:13 NIV). "Joshua asked, "Why did you bring this people across the Jordan to deliver us into the hands of the Amorites to destroy us?'" (Josh. 7:7 NIV). Nehemiah asked, "Why is the house of God forsaken?"

(Neh.13:11 NKJV). Job asked, "Why have you made me your target?" (Job 7:20 NIV). King David cried, "My God, why have you forsaken me?" (Ps. 22:1 NIV). And we know David's cry was the same as our Lord from the cross when He cried "My God, My God, why have you forsaken me" (Matt. 27:46 NIV).

We all would do well to remember our Lord's cry. Because of Christ's cry on Calvary the believer never has to make that cry. God's Word and promise is true yesterday, today, and forever. He will never leave us nor forsake us. We may not know what the good is from this test, but He does. What we do know is that the cross is the answer and victory to all fears and questions to those who love God. The cross tells the called that we can trust Him in all circumstances and that what we see dimly and perhaps fearfully today, will be fully understood with glory someday. Our faith commands us to trust that our circumstances will work together for our good.

Like that fateful time in New York decades ago, when we see empty streets across the world or feel empty inside or see a virus taking thousands of lives or see millions of people losing their jobs never forget how Romans 8 ends:

> Can anything separate us from Christ's love? Can trouble or problems or persecution separate us from his love? If we have no food or clothes or face danger or even death, will that separate us from his love? As the Scriptures say, "For you we are in danger of death all the time. People think we are worth no more than sheep to be killed." But in all these troubles we have complete victory through God, who has shown his love for us. Yes, I am sure that nothing can separate us from God's love—not death, life, angels, or ruling spirits. I am sure that nothing now, nothing in the future, no powers, nothing above us or nothing below us—nothing in the whole created world—will ever be able to separate us from the love God has shown us in Christ Jesus our Lord. (Rom. 8:35–39 ERV)

THOUGHTS

_____

_____

_____

_____

_____

_____

_____

PRAYER

_____

_____

_____

_____

_____

_____

_____

DAY 2

"Continue in prayer, and watch in the same with thanksgiving; Withal praying also for us, that God would open unto us a door of utterance, to speak the mystery of Christ, for which I am also in bonds: That I may make it manifest, as I ought to speak. Walk in wisdom toward them that are without, redeeming the time. Let your speech be always with grace, seasoned with salt, that ye may know how ye ought to answer every man."

—Colossians 4:2–6 (KJV)

DILIGENT ACTIONS OF FAITH

IN TODAY'S PASSAGE Paul provides three practical applications of faith. As believers we must be

1. Diligent in prayer,
2. Diligent in wisdom, and
3. Diligent in speech.

Diligent in Prayer

It is essential for believers to be diligent prayer warriors to live a victorious life in Christ. In verse 2, Paul says we must "continue in prayer." The word *continue* implies devoting our lives to prayer. It is to pursue earnestly, with perseverance and diligence, in order to be effective. It is waiting on the Lord. Prayer must be diligently pursued and should be our passion. As John Bunyan said, prayer will make you leave off sinning, or sinning will make you leave off prayer.

Paul then says to "watch with Thanksgiving." The idea is to stay alert. This is needed for an effective prayer life. We need to be alert to the spiritual matters around us, praying in the moment not in the mundane. The word *watch* is the same word Jesus used when talking to the disciples in the garden of Gethsemane before His arrest. We know how that turned out. Stay alert beloved.

Know what's going on around you and pray accordingly—and with thanksgiving. Our hearts are to be grateful for the love and promises we have in Christ Jesus.

In verses 3 and 4 Paul tells us the specifics of his prayers. He prays for an open door for the gospel to be shared. A good prayer for any servant of God. Paul did not let the fact that he was in prison because of his faith and ministry hinder his prayer life. He was not praying for matters of the flesh, not for comfort, a way out, but rather for the love of God to be shared throughout Rome.

Diligent in Wisdom

The second practical application for believers to act on is to be diligent in wisdom. King Solomon' wrote that it is better to "get wisdom than gold" (Pro. 16:16 NIV). As believers we need wisdom to navigate the ways and issues of life in order to live victoriously in Christ. We need godly wisdom to be better husbands, wives, siblings, employees, employers, and better servants of God as we are called to share among those without.

And Paul says to "walk circumspectly, not as fools but as wise, redeeming the time" (Eph. 5:15–16 KJV). Those in Christ need to make the most of our time in kingdom work. We are not to be idle in the time we are given here on earth. As someone once said: "Yesterday is a cashed check, tomorrow is a promissory note, today is cash in hand. Use it well. Invest today."

Diligent in Speech

The third practical application Paul shares is to be diligent in speech found in verse 6. People need love and truth now more than ever. A Christian's speech should reflect the reverence of grace we've received in our heart and grace is manifested in the words we speak. Our words can transform lives and situations. Echoing the Lord, Paul says our words need to be seasoned with salt. Our words need to enhance a taste and thirst for the truth and words need to be preserving truth. Leave them wanting more and share the truth in love (Eph. 4:15). Martin Luther said "Faith, like light, should always be simple and unbending; while love, like warmth, should beam forth on every side, and bend to every necessity of our brethren." Be diligent in your speech as this is the answer people seek.

So my friends, let the love of God manifest victoriously in your lives as you are diligent in prayer, diligent in wisdom, and diligent in speech. In Jesus's name. Amen.

THOUGHTS

_____

_____

_____

_____

_____

_____

_____

PRAYER

_____

_____

_____

_____

_____

_____

_____

DAY 3

"Faith is what makes real the things we hope for.
It is proof of what we cannot see."

—Hebrews 11:1 (ERV)

ONE DEGREE OF heat is the difference between hot and boiling water. A few inches can determine the outcome of a football game. One stroke can determine a PGA championship. One split second can bring victory in a NASCAR race. So too can one more degree, one more measure, one extra determination means the difference between spiritual victory or defeat in our faith relationship with God.

Chapter 11 of the book of Hebrews is what some have called the Hall of Faith as it testifies to the degrees and measures and determinations of faith in action with biblical heroes such as Abel, Enoch, Noah, Abraham, Sara, Isaac, Jacob, Joseph, Rahab, Gideon, Samson, David, and many others who through faith defeated kingdoms and exhibited righteousness in the midst of opposition, the weak being made strong and the deliverance of many from imminent death.

The great promise to believers today is that all can access the same faith of these heroes. Our verse speaks to faith as the foundation of what we believe: our hope that someday this life will be gone, and we have an inheritance from God and our Lord Jesus Christ of an eternal life incorruptible and undefiled. The second half of the verse tells us our faith is the evidence (proof) of things unseen. The Greek word here means conviction. Our faith is exercised in and through the conviction of what we believe. Faith will be manifested in everyday life with decisions, patience and trust based on the promises we know, not what we see. C. S. Lewis wrote "If you read history, you will find that the Christians who did most for the present world were precisely those who thought most of the next world."

As we face the challenges of the world today, what does your faith look like? The Bible gives numerous examples of those with no faith and those with little faith and those with great faith. Where are you on that scale right now? It is faith that pleases God (11:6). And there is great blessing attached to faith (11:3). How solid is your foundation and what is the conviction of your faith right now? Perhaps you need to turn your faith up a degree, a good measure, or that action you have been putting off. The Bible says the just shall live by faith (Rom. 1:17). Let us all prayerfully consider and create our own hero of faith testimony.

THOUGHTS

_____

_____

_____

_____

_____

_____

PRAYER

_____

_____

_____

_____

_____

_____

DAY 4

"Everything that breathes, praise the LORD! Praise the LORD!"

—Psalm 150:6 (ERV)

THE DEFINITION OF *praise* is to honor and ascribe worth to something. In this case we are to praise God. It is the response due to God because of His majesty and saving action to His creation and should dominate one's character as the proof of true reverence for God. As with prayer, praise changes things.

Psalm 150 is the great exclamation point to the end of what is known as the hallelujah Psalms, which begin with Psalm 146. It is the great outburst of rejoicing in song from God's people in homage to an amazing God. What a scene this would have been back in the day. There was an orchestra of perhaps some four thousand musicians each playing an instrument said to have been made by King David himself (1 Chron. 23:5). There were the stringed instruments of the harps and dulcimers.

Like in the temple with the thousands of worshippers, the totality of Psalm 150 instructs us to praise God everywhere (v. 1). We are to praise Him because of all the great things He does and because God is great (v. 2). We are to praise Him with voices and instruments (vv. 3–5) and as we live and breathe, we are to praise the Lord thy God (v. 6). But what about times when we don't feel praise in our hearts? When circumstances and darkness have overwhelmed us and quenched the joy in our heart and sapped us of the strength to praise the Lord? Years ago, I discovered a great blessing at the end of the book of Psalms. Prior to the praise of song beginning in Psalm 146, we find psalms of prayer. It is prayer that can lead us out of darkness and into great rejoicing again. When down and out; when weak and low; when despairing, anxious, or hopeless I find myself going back to Psalm 140 and reading the beginning verses of each psalm through 149 before reading all of Psalm 150. From the prayers of circumstance to rejoicing, I read until the great crescendo of praise in Psalm 150 as it brings flight to the heart.

In the color of the King James language, we plead in prayer:

"Deliver me, O Lord, from the evil man: preserve me from the violent man" (140:1). "Keep me, O Lord, from the hands of the wicked" (140:4).

"Lord, I cry unto thee: make haste unto me; give ear unto my voice when I cry unto thee" (141:1). "I cried unto the Lord with my voice; with my voice unto the Lord did I make supplication" (142:1).

"Hear my prayer, O Lord, give ear to my supplications; in thy faithfulness answer me, and in the thy righteousness" (143:1).

Extol such great promises

"Blessed be the Lord my strength … my goodness, and my fortress; my high tower, and my deliverer; my shield, and he in whom I trust" (144:1–2).

"I will extol thee, my God, O king; and I will bless thy name for ever and ever" (145:1).

We sing it out loud in praise

"Praise ye the Lord. Praise the Lord, O my soul. While I live will I praise the Lord: I will sing praises unto my God while I have any being" (146:1–2).

"Praise ye the Lord: for it is good to sing praises unto our God" (147:1).

"Praise ye the Lord, Praise ye the Lord from the heavens: praise him in the heights" (148:1).

"Praise ye the Lord. Sing unto the Lord a new song, and his praise in the congregation of saints" (149:1).

And the anthem of praise! When we pull out our Bic lighters (old school days), or cell phones and turn your lights on, and sing out loud and dance with me:

"Praise ye the LORD. Praise God in His sanctuary: praise him in the firmament of his power. Praise him for his mighty acts: praise him according to His excellent greatness. Praise him with the sound of the trumpet: praise him with the psaltery and harp. Praise him with the timbrel and dance: praise him with stringed instruments and organs. Praise him upon the loud cymbals: praise him upon the high sounding cymbals. Let everything that hath breath praise the LORD! Praise ye the LORD.

Are you feeling better in the heart? Is your joy renewed? He is always worthy of our praise and remember whether we feel like praising or not there will be praise. Jesus said that even if the people remain silent, "the stones will cry out" (Luke 19:40 NIV). Don't let a stone take the place of your blessing for lack of praise. Pray yourself into praise today. Knowing you are an overcomer of circumstances and there is always victory in Jesus Christ!

THOUGHTS

PRAYER

DAY 5

"Arise, shine, for your light has come, and the glory of the LORD has risen upon you. For behold, darkness shall cover the earth, and thick darkness the peoples; but the LORD will arise upon you and His glory will be seen upon you."

—Isaiah 60:1–2 (ESV)

WE HAVE HERE the great prophecy concerning the promise of our Lord's return, reign, and redemption of His people and His city, Jerusalem. The promise comes at a time of great suffering for God's people. They have been in the lengthy darkness of exile from their beloved city, Jerusalem. Even so, much of the city lies in ruins.

We have seen in recent years so much the same as God's people are feeling the same emotions. With all the political tensions, crime, killings, protests, and turmoil, the news is full of pain and misery. If you are like me, you may be feeling exasperated and despairing of so much of what we see across our cities. They are many of the same emotions God's people were experiencing at the time of Isaiah's prophecy. As with God's people in our passage, our Lord does not allow circumstances destroy His people, but rather He uses circumstances to redeem His people. I sense the literal light of Isaiah's prophecy is around the corner. The glory of Yahweh is upon us! Maranatha is in our near future!

Until then, we are here in this moment, and as His people we have a purpose. I want to focus for a moment on the word *arise*. We have been promised that the Lord will arise. His light will shine. Glory will come to His people. Nevertheless, the instruction and application for us today to receive this promise and the gift of redemption is that as His people we must arise. ARISE! SHINE! God's people, the church, now more than ever needs to stand up and be seen and heard. It is not a religious arising, nor is it a cultural arising. Rather, it should be a relationship arising. It is about our own relationship with God, and our relationships with others through God. "God's people must rise up physically, emotionally, and spiritually "for such a time as this" (Esther 4:14) if this country and world is to be healed and redeemed of this great awakening of sins and injustices.

Dr. John Perkins, in his book *One Blood, Parting Words to the Church on Race*, said: "There is no institution on earth more equipped or more capable of bringing transformation to the cause of reconciliation than the church." We rise up in conviction not condemnation. The conviction of His truth for spiritual justice. We rise up individually and corporately to engage this world with Jesus. To be great witnesses of His light and glory. Jesus is the one who will bring true change and healing the world needs.

Allow me to leave you with words of encouragement, or conviction, depending on where your heart and relationship with God is. It comes from Charles Spurgeon saying "I am afraid for you who go ankle deep into religion and never venture further—I am afraid lest you should, by-and-by, return to the shore! But as for you who plunge into the center of the stream and find waters to swim in, I have no fears! You shall be borne onward by a current ever increasing in strength, till in the ocean of eternal love you shall lose yourselves in Heaven above!"

Now is the time church. ARISE! SHINE! All of this will pass one way or another. Best to jump in the stream and enjoy the flow.

THOUGHTS

_____

_____

_____

_____

_____

_____

_____

PRAYER

_____

_____

_____

_____

_____

_____

_____

DAY 6

"Now when these things begin to happen, look up and lift up your heads, because your redemption draws near."

—Luke 21:28 (NKJV)

THE "THINGS JESUS refers to in our passage are the events (signs) leading to the coming of our Lord. Our Redeemer's return to rule and reign. Beginning in verse 25 of the chapter Jesus speaks about great global upheavals. It is a warning. There will be catastrophic cosmic and environmental events. There will be distresses among nations and people. Confusion and perplexity will rule the day. People will be at their wits end as the world will be morally bankrupt. Anxiety, panic, and fear will grip people's hearts and minds.

Are we there yet? The Bible tells us that no one knows the day or hour of our Lord's return (Matt. 24:36), but it sure seems to me like redemption is close. Whether today, tomorrow, next year, next decade, what is important for the believer to grasp is to be ready now. In all the turmoil that seems to be going on in the world we are not to be afraid or cowering, but rather we are to stand up with our heads high for truth and righteousness, knowing the Lord could arrive at any time—living with a "look up" perspective as our redemption is near. The Greek word for "look up" speaks to looking with an outstretched neck. The idea is we should be living with an eternal perspective in great anticipation of our Lord's coming. It is much the same sentiment as Paul wrote to the Philippians: "I press toward the mark for the prize of the high calling of God in Christ Jesus" (Phil. 3:14 KJV). The mark is the finish line in a race, and we should be pressing with outstretched neck to win the gold medal.

With political chaos reigning, heroes being canceled and replaced by celebrity only to be canceled eventually themselves, policy being formed by "likes," all that is popular and all the talk of the town today, can be gone tomorrow. Anything and everything the world has to offer, good and bad, is only temporal. But as Jesus says, "heaven and earth will pass away, but my words will by no means pass away" (Luke 21:33 NIV). We are to live our lives with an eternal perspective grounded in the supremacy and authority of Jesus Christ.

As crazy as the world seems to be and seems to be becoming, Christians need not cower in fear. The signs reveal the King is on the way. He tells us to have joy because our redemption draws near. So remember, beloved, to always look up!

THOUGHTS

_____

_____

_____

_____

_____

PRAYER

_____

_____

_____

_____

_____

DAY 7

*"The soldiers were going out of the city with Jesus.
They saw a man from Cyrene named Simon, and they
forced him to carry Jesus' cross."*

—Matthew 27:32 (ERV)

THIS VERSE REMINDS me of the scene from the movie *The Passion of the Christ* when the procession arrives at Calvary. In the scene the Roman soldiers tell Simon of Cyrene to run along, and we see Simon on the edge of the cliff, starring back toward Jesus in complete awe before he runs away.

I so look forward to meeting Simon in heaven. He was a special chosen vessel of God. Whereas Adam is the first of creation, Abraham is the father of faith, Mary is the one and only mother of Jesus, Simon is the only one who walked with Jesus, carrying His cross, likely mocked and spit upon as they proceeded to the place of the skull. I want to know what Jesus personally said to Simon on the way to Calvary in their shared agony. Words reserved only for a testimony in eternity.

We all have a destiny with eternity. Simon's destiny with eternity in bearing the cross of Jesus is unique but not exclusive. We all have or will have an encounter with the cross of Jesus. The question is what have we done or what will we do with it? Simon was forced by the soldiers to carry the cross with Jesus (Luke 23:26). I have a feeling he protested. "Why me? I am not a condemned man. I am a righteous man." However, the Bible is very clear there is none righteous, no not one (Rom. 3:10), except Jesus (1 John 2:1). You see Simon represents all of us in unrighteousness because of sin. And all of us need a true encounter with Jesus and the cross. As Simon ran off that cliff to reunite with his family, sweaty and defiled, rather than able to celebrate the Passover with family, he would have to go through a ceremonial cleansing process. For Simon this would become his new Passover, most likely recalling the words of Jesus and his encounter with the cross. Perhaps along the way to Calvary Jesus said to Simon, "Come unto me, Simon, as you are weary and heavy laden. I will give you rest. Learn from Me and follow Me, and I will give you rest for your soul."

The Bible tells us the cross is a place of substitution as Jesus took our place for the judgment and punishment of our sin (1 John 2:2). The cross is the place of separation that sets apart the believer from the world (1 Pet. 2:9–10). The cross is also the place of victory over death and Satan's hold on us (1 Cor. 15:54–57). And the cross is the end and the new beginning to those who believe (2 Cor. 5:17). Simon's cross encounter changed him and his family forever. We have the glorious testimony in Mark 15:21 of Rufus and Alexander, followers of Jesus whose father was Simon. Many scholars believe this to be Simon of Cyrene. And Paul even sends greetings to his fellow Christian brothers, Rufus and Alexander, and their mother in his letter to the Romans (16:13). Simon could not partake in the Passover after his encounter with Jesus and the cross. However, he had a new Passover story to share with his family. A better Passover. A complete Passover.

Simon did not have a choice when forced to confront the cross of Jesus. You and I do have that choice. For those who have never chosen the cross and the way of Jesus, today is the day, now is the acceptable time. Repent of your sin. Receive God's love and forgiveness and give and surrender your life to Christ as Savior and Lord. Be filled with the Holy Spirit to be a glorious witness for Him in these last days rejoicing in your new covenant, your new Passover.

For those who have encountered the cross and surrendered their lives to Jesus as new creations in Christ, perhaps this is a day to reflect and revere what it means, and the price Jesus paid for your salvation. The cross of Jesus is what defines Simon of Cyrene. Does it define you?

THOUGHTS

_____

_____

_____

_____

_____

_____

_____

PRAYER

_____

_____

_____

_____

_____

_____

_____

DAY 8

"Then Boaz said to the elders and all the people; '
you are witnesses today that I am buying from Naomi
everything that belonged to Elimelech, Kilion, and Mahlon.
I also took Ruth to be my wife.'"

—Ruth 4:9–10 (ERV)

AT THE END of the book of Ruth we see the completion of Ruth and her mother-in-law's' redemption. They are in the process of returning to Bethlehem, the house of bread. Both their husbands have died, yet Ruth chose to serve Naomi rather than return to her people and their god. We see a beautiful process of God's redemptive work as they labor in their faith, eventually coming to a place of rest as Ruth waits on Boaz in marriage and giving Naomi a place in the family in this divine matrimony.

Boaz steps in as the kinsmen redeemer after the rightful eldest kinsmen backed out. Boaz buys back Naomi's family's land. In the fullness of God's glory Boaz is a type of Christ, who is our Kinsmen redeemer. Our Jehovah, Goel (Redeemer), who willingly substituted Himself in our place, taking on Himself our death as judgement for sin. He shed His blood to redeem and purchase earth and humankind back to God from Satan's rule. Boaz emulates the heart of Christ in that he has a heart *not* for the field but first and foremost for the bride. His desire was to have Ruth in marriage, and the property was the blessing to bring joy and peace into not only her life but Naomi's as well. Such is the heart of Christ for you and me. He is not worried about the world. His day will come. Jesus is more concerned today about your heart and salvation and that you enter into His joy and the marriage supper of the lamb. Christ's concern is for the spiritual health of His bride, the church. Such should be the heart of every believer. We are to love and care for one another as Christ cares for His people and His church.

Although Naomi and Ruth suffered much sorrow and difficulty, they were redeemed to heavenly heights neither could ever imagine. The bloodline of Christ comes from the marriage of Ruth and Boaz, and Naomi was along for the blessing of caring and raising their child. "Eye has not seen, nor ear heard, Nor have entered into the heart of man The things which God has prepared for those who love Him" (1 Cor. 2:9 NKJV). From the beginning of the book, Naomi is seen as hopeless and empty. But in the end her land and life are redeemed, and her heart has been transformed from bitterness to rejoicing. Ruth, the astounding picture of faith, chose to sacrifice her life and her goals and desires to serve her mother-in-law. In the end we see God's redemptive work leading her into a place of rest and a blessed marriage and new family.

Who is your Redeemer? Who is your Savior? Your Jehovah-Goel? Where does your help come from? "The kingdom of heaven is like treasure hidden in a field, which a man found and hid; and for joy over it he goes and sells all that he has and buys that field" (Matt 13:44 NKJV). Jesus gave everything He had to redeem His treasure, His field, you and me. We are bought by His blood from the corruption of sin and its sentence to hell to the redeemed promise of eternal life and His blessings for today.

THOUGHTS

PRAYER

DAY 9

"Simon Peter replied, 'LORD to whom would we go? "
You alone have the words that give eternal life."'

—John 6:68 (NLT)

PETER, A PILLAR of the early church, was strong, bold, zealous, devoted, courageous, generous, a gifted leader, loyal, and possessing a warm heart. He was also rash, impulsive, at times disrespectful, and selfish. Early twentieth-century Scottish Presbyterian minister George H. Morrison says of Peter: "One recognizes the slumbering greatness of him, but one also feels the boundless possibilities of evil. But Jesus handles him and plays upon him as a master musician might play on his loved instrument, till the chords are wakened into such a glorious music that the centuries are ringing with it still."

The apostle John records an event when Peter' expresses the hope he has in Jesus. The scene is following the miraculous feeding of the five thousand. It was so great a miracle the people practically demand Jesus set up His kingdom right then and there. But the Lord's time had not come yet and instead He taught on a suffering Messiah rather than a conquering Messiah and on the "bread of life," which was a truth the people were not willing to receive. So the crowd of some fifteen thousand, including women and children, turned away from Christ. That is when Jesus turns to Peter and James and Andrew and Phillip and the rest of the disciples and asks, "'do you also want to go away?' But Simon Peter answered Him, 'Lord, to whom shall we go? You have the words of eternal life'" (John 6:67–68 NKJV).

Hope and comfort in this life is not found in places or world kingdoms and ways, but rather in the One who gave us the Word of eternal life. It is easy to say one follows Christ when times are good, when there is plenty of fish and bread and merriment.

However, real faith is on display when one runs to Christ when the going is tough. When we lose a job or struggle to make ends meet. When a marriage is falling apart, or we are in despair over a prodigal child. When facing unexpected illness or death of a loved one. To whom shall you go? To whom shall you go when the Word of God challenges our hearts to change as one struggles with pride or selfishness? To whom shall you go when persecution and spiritual warfare is unrelenting? The only answer is Jesus because only He has the true words that provide truth and hope and comfort that Father God designed each of our hearts and souls to receive. Peter's profound yet simple declaration reminds us that nothing in the world has the true answers to life and nothing of the world can help us in our divine process of faith and that nothing in this world provides the answers to eternity. Jesus, the Word, who was with God from the beginning of it all and who is God and through whom all things were created and in whom is life, became human and dwelt among us (John 1:1–14), and that Jesus is the way, the truth, the life, and no one comes to the Father except through Him (John 14:6).

Peter was so fabulous in his faith as well as his flaws. He made many missteps in his walk with the Lord, including denying Jesus three times before the rooster crowed (John 18:25–27). Peter ran away in shame in that moment, but he never turned his heart away from Jesus. And the Word of eternal life was always there for Peter. The angel at the tomb said to the women, "go and tell the disciples, *and Peter*, 'He is going ahead of you into Galilee'" (Mark 16:7 NIV, emphasis mine). Paul tells us it was Peter whom Jesus first appeared to after the resurrection and then the twelve (1 Cor. 15:5). And when they had finished eating by the shores of the Sea of Galilee, the Lord' restored Peter and his ministry as a fisher of souls (John 21:15–25).

Jesus was Peter's Savior, his mentor, and his friend. Peter's faith was forged and tempered by the eternal words of love and grace. He would faithfully minister to his end. Church tradition tells us Peter was forced to watch his wife be crucified, during which he shouted, "remember, Dear, our Lord!" And when it came time for his death, Peter told his persecutors to crucify him upside down, as he was not worthy to die in the same manner as his Lord.

To whom shall you go, friend? Peter represents the hope and comfort we all can have in Jesus Christ, no matter our circumstance. Run to the loving arms of Jesus who alone has words of eternal life, and you shall have victory! He and He alone is the Shepard and Overseer of our souls (1 Pet. 2:25).

THOUGHTS

PRAYER

DAY 10

*"My people have done two things. They turned away from Me,
and they dug their own cisterns. I am the source of living water;
these cisterns are broken and cannot hold water."*

—Jeremiah 2:13 (ERV)

JEREMIAH WAS KNOWN as the weeping prophet. His words
fell on hard hearts, leaving him distraught and depressed. He was
preaching during the time of the fall of Jerusalem as the brightest
and leading citizens were taken captive by the Babylonians. He
would have witnessed the ransacking and destruction of the
great city and the suffering of his people. He watched as the
consequences of sin became more profound and pronounced as
his people slipped further and further away from God, rejecting
Yahweh's way and the call to repent.

Jeremiah's journey actually began with hope under King
Josiah's rule with a movement of political and religious reform.
A wide populous supported this movement. Jeremiah was probably on board as well. However, he soon became disillusioned
and began preaching against the movement that had become
dreadfully wrong and ungodly. The people turned from the one
true God to a nation worshipping the many gods of the land of
Canaan—the false gods of fertility, pleasure, power, and prosperity—the false gods of religious, political, and social causes
usurping the cause of God. Jeremiah warned against the rampant
injustices, corruption, and social evils with the religious and
political leaders leading the charge to effectively out-pagan the
pagans of the day.

Many believe politics has no place in Christian faith.
Certainly, we find the message of Jesus was that of regeneration
of the heart, mind, and soul. And yet politics and religion played
a major part of His ministry. His public ministry took to the

streets after the political arrest of John the Baptist. His message was political in that it was about a coming kingdom of God as opposed to the kingdom of Rome or King Herod's kingdom. He passionately spoke of God's love and character in stark contrast to the religious and political leaders of the day. His crucifixion on a Roman cross was political in and of itself.

Christians today must not lose hope with all the political and religious troubles inundating the world today. Like Jeremiah, in spite of all the darkness, we have witnessed the faithfulness of God. People can reject God and mock His truth, but that has never stopped God from speaking. The Lord continues to warn His people when they go astray. His love continually calls people to repent and come back to Him. God's plan for His people is true today as it was yesterday and will be tomorrow. As Christians, we are in a battle for righteousness on a scale like never before. We must endure to the end and stand tall for righteousness and right living.

Let me dip into the political and religious world of a time past with a quote from Martin Niemoller, a pastor opposed to the Nazi regime's intrusion into the affairs of the church. From the pulpit in 1934 Pastor Niemoller said, "We have all of us—the whole church and the whole community—we've been thrown into the Tempter's sieve, and he is shaking and the wind is blowing, and it must now become manifest whether we are wheat or chaff! Verily, a time of sifting has come upon us, and even the most indolent and peaceful person among us must see that the calm of a meditative Christianity is at an end. . . . . It is now springtime for the hopeful and expectant Christian Church—it is testing time, and God is giving Satan a free hand, so he may shake us up and so that it may be seen what manner of people we are. . . . Satan swings his sieve and Christianity is thrown hither and thither, and he who is not ready to suffer, who calls himself a Christian only because he thereby hoped to gain something good for his race and his nation is blown away like chaff by the wind of time."

Are we as Christians facing such a challenge from God today? Politics and religion have become dreadful tools as a means to political, economic, and social ends. But politics and religion will never be the solution, only more broken cisterns. Jesus alone is the answer for today. He is the solution and source of living water for all things godly and good. For Christians the time is now to regain the higher ground of His love. The higher ground of grace and mercy. The higher ground of the cross, no matter the cost. There are battles to fight. Losses to endure. But in the end, we know who wins the war. Soldier on beloved of Christ! Rise up and fight the good fight of faith!

THOUGHTS

PRAYER

DAY 11

"Don't be afraid what will happen to you. I tell you, the devil will put some of you in prison. He will do this to test you. You will suffer for ten days, but be faithful, even if you have to die. If you continue to be faithful, I will give you the reward of life."

—Revelation 2:10 (ERV)

OUR PASSAGE FINDS John receiving the second of seven letters to the New Testament church from Jesus. It is the letter to the persecuted church in Smyrna where Christians were suffering for refusing to worship Caesar. Jesus began the letter commending the church for the good fruits of their works and ministry. He then acknowledges their tribulations and suffering for believing and standing for the gospel truth. He knows their "poverty or "beggary, as the Greek portrays it. The Christians in Smyrna were reduced to begging in the streets for their very existence. Ostracized from family and friends for their beliefs, having no work, being rejected by the trade unions, they had nothing. But Jesus sees it all, and He cares for them.

The devil says God does not care about you or your suffering. But truth is God does care, and our Lord will never leave you nor forsake you. And in 'the letter to the persecuted church in Smyrna, Jesus moves from a commendation of their good works and care of their suffering to the remedy for their situation. He says, "don't be afraid . . . but be faithful." Fear not and be faithful is the exhortation. It is the same remedy He gives to all Christians through the ages—even to today: Fear not and be faithful. After rescuing Lot and fearing death, God reassured Abram and said, "Fear not, Abram, I am thy shield, and thy exceeding great reward" (Gen. 15:1 KJV). Paul, exhorting Christians in Corinth, declares, "it is required in' stewards that one be found faithful" (1 Cor. 4:2 NKJV). The ten days of suffering in our passage speaks to something bad coming, but there will also be an end to it. The remedy remains the same: fear not and be faithful.

It is this remedy that ultimately leads to the fulfillment of our Lord's promise. He will give the faithful the "reward of life." The crown of life, the promise of heaven. So beloved in Christ, whatever trial or trouble or suffering you face press on with the good works you have been called to do (Phil. 3:14). Keep fighting the good fight of faith (1 Tim. 6:12). Fear not and know that if God be for you, who can be against you (Rom. 8:31), and that in spite of trials and tribulations, persecution, pandemics, and uncertainty in uncertain times, know you are just passing through on your way to glory (1 Chron. 29:15). To an inheritance incorruptible, undefiled, that never fades away, reserved in heaven for the faithful, being guarded by the power of God through faith for a salvation ready to be revealed in the last time (1 Pet. 1:4–5). And when you get there may you hear the words of our Lord say, "well done good and faithful servant" (Matt. 25:23 NKJV).

THOUGHTS

_____

_____

_____

_____

_____

_____

PRAYER

_____

_____

_____

_____

_____

_____

DAY 12

"God is spirit, so the people who worship Him
must worship in spirit and truth."

—John 4:24 (ESV)

IN THE TESTIMONY of the Samaritan woman at the well we have an example of religion being one of the most common excuses in refusing the true God. Whether it be from a moralist such as Nicodemus or an immoralist such as the Samaritan woman, people want to justify sin by saying one is religious. "I go to church, so I'm good with God," is a feeble expression of religion, but they know not what they truly worship.

Jesus says, "the time is coming when the true worshipers will worship the Father in spirit and truth" (John 4:23 ERV). Later Jesus says, "I am the way, and the truth, and the life. No one comes to the Father except through me," (John 14:6 ESV), a reference to His deity and the way of salvation, truth, and life. By saying to the Samaritan woman that "people who worship Him must worship in spirit and truth" takes the Samaritan woman's false religious theology out of the realm of time and space and makes it a matter of the heart with God. The woman was using her worship of god as a cover for her immoral life. But it was not a true worship of the heart. True worship of God will move from an action of the flesh to an expression of the heart, creating a sense of reverence and fear that will turn from immoral actions. Job is described as one who feared God and eschewed evil (Job 1:1). One's true worship of God will compel a reverent fear of God giving one a corresponding fear of evil. Jesus said, "do not fear those who kill the body but cannot kill the soul. But rather fear Him who is able to destroy both soul and body in hell" (Matt 10:28 NKJV).

To worship God is to worship Him in spirit and truth. To worship in spirit is to worship from the heart, in fear and sincerity of heart not from formality and out of religious obligation. To worship in truth is to worship in and through the true way of God. True worship is not a religious activity, but rather a real relationship with God through Jesus Christ who is the only mediator between God and us (1 Tim. 2:5). To worship in spirit and truth will result in a healthy and glorious fear of an awesome God.

So, beloved of Christ, check your worship if it is in spirit and truth. Make sure it is personal in relationship with Jesus Christ, spiritual in heart, intellectual but also emotional in fear and reverence. Make sure it is worship that is manifested in sincere responses of adoration, praise, love, sacrifice, obedience of a life lived in God through Jesus Christ our Lord.

THOUGHTS

_____

_____

_____

_____

_____

_____

_____

PRAYER

_____

_____

_____

_____

_____

_____

_____

DAY 13

"The following night the Lord stood by Paul, and said:
"Be of good cheer, Paul: for as thou hast testified of me in
Jerusalem, so must thou bear witness also in Rome."

—Acts 23:11 (KJV)

PAUL IS SITTING in a Jerusalem barracks. Imprisoned, suffering from almost being torn to shreds by a mob, beaten, rejected, alone, and isolated in a dank, dark prison cell. But God, the Lord Jesus makes an appearance to Paul. Cheer up Paul! Be of good courage! I promised to get you to Rome, and My promises never go void.

Isolation is perhaps the worst that can happen to a Christian. Such a condition is the playground for the enemy to attack with loneliness, discouragement, despair, anxiety, and hopelessness. Isolation can often lead to cynicism, paranoia, fear, anger, bitterness, depression, and other ailments that affects not only one's spiritual health, but also one's witness and relationship with the Lord. Isolation negatively affects the spirit, mind, body, and soul. It can often be self-inflicted in a world that seemingly gives us access to everything. Social media, for example, has caused so many people, as well as Christians, to feel isolated and lonely as one becomes obsessed with "likes" and falls into tribalism and seeking worldly remedies for relationships and peace of mind and heart that never lasts. Here in California we have a popular fast-food chain called In-N-Out Burger that serves up a tasty take on burgers, fries, and shakes. Someone once said: "Social media is like having an In-N-Out franchise in your own garage open 24/7 365 Always available, never having to leave, but that does not necessarily make it a good thing."

God did not create people to be isolated. Our Lord's appearance to Paul in our text emphasizes that in times of isolation and loneliness, the best remedy starts with Jesus. In his isolation

Paul thought he was a failure for the Lord. His testimony has been rejected, and his heart's desire was to get to Rome to testify of Jesus and share the gospel to those he loved and knew well (Rom. 1:9–12). It all seemed hopelessly impossible. But Jesus. As Christians we are required to bring Christ to people, not people to Christ. We are called to till the ground, sow the seed, water and nourish, and the Lord will provide the fruits of increase to His kingdom. Jesus exhorts Paul to cheer up, have courage, to know that his witness was well pleasing to the Lord. He is saying I'll take it from here and don't worry about your dark circumstances, because as I promised, I will get you to Rome.

The point is God never fails. Even when we feel isolated or lonely. As long as we keep looking up and seeking Him it will all be okay. Joshua, isolated in his thoughts and fearing his ability to lead the nation of Israel, was comforted by the Lord: "be strong and of good courage; for you shall bring the people of Israel into the land of which I swore to them, and I will be with you" (Duet. 31:23 NKJV). In Isaiah's time of isolation and fear the Lord God appeared and said: "fear not, for I am with you; be not dismayed for I am your God. I will strengthen you, yes, I will help you, yes, I will uphold you with My righteous right hand" (Isa. 41:10 NKJV). I can't help but wonder if Peter thought of this Scripture as Jesus reached His hand out to keep him from sinking in the water.

Jesus tells God's people: "I am with you always, even to the end of the age" (Matt. 28:20 NKJV). As Jesus was with Paul, so He is with His people, you and me today. Whenever we are discouraged, despairing, in the low valleys of life, rejected and isolated, the promise always is the same: He will never leave us nor forsake us (Heb. 13:5). The promise was settled and sealed at the cross, so remember your call as a beloved child of God. Pastors, teachers, all servants of God, go and get it! Claim your mission field. Pursue all with passion and continue to always look to Jesus whose right hand will always be there to lift us out of the despair of isolation and loneliness. Trust that Father God knows best and has His best for you.

THOUGHTS

_____

_____

_____

_____

_____

_____

_____

PRAYER

_____

_____

_____

_____

_____

_____

_____

DAY 14

"But you are a chosen generation, a royal priesthood,
a holy nation, His own special people, that you may proclaim
the praises of Him who called you out of darkness and
into His marvelous light."

—1 Peter 2:9 (NKJV)

IN PETER'S FIRST letter to the churches of Asia Minor, he wrote of the foundation of the temple as being representative of Jesus Christ and His ministry as the chief cornerstone of our salvation, righteousness, and holiness. In other words, Jesus Christ is the chief cornerstone of the believers' faith.

Peter, referencing Psalm 118:22, testifies of how the chief cornerstone of the temple was rejected and thrown aside during the building process (1 Pet. 2:7–8). It is a sad picture of Christ being rejected by Israel. In the book of Acts we read about the healing of a lame man. Afterward, Peter is brought before the religious rulers who ask, "by what power and by whose name" have you healed this man? Peter testifies that Jesus is the stone rejected by the builders, which is the (chief) cornerstone and there is salvation in no other name (Acts 4:7–12).

There is a day of visitation in everyone's life and everyone's heart for which Jesus will be either a stumbling stone or a rock of salvation and a precious cornerstone of one's faith and life. The stumbling stone gets in the way of self-prescribed religions and worldly worship and is rejected. However, as the precious corner-stone, Christ is received by faith and brings everlasting salvation and righteousness, holiness, and truth to those who believe.

We are the cornerstone people. And in our passage Peter tells us as cornerstone people we are a chosen generation, a favored generation. We are a royal priesthood, representatives, and instruments of God's kingdom. Cornerstone people are a holy nation; we are separated and set apart from this world. We are His own special people; we are God's own under His divine and direct care and attention and love and grace, and we navigate this world in and through the light of Christ. What an awesome blessing to be in the family of cornerstone people!

Peter also reminds us that there is responsibility attached to being such people. We are called to praise our Lord. We are to "proclaim our praises. Our faith is not to be hidden under a bushel but rather to be shouted and lived out loud so a dark world can see the light of a loving God. It is a marvelous light, holy and divine. And as the psalmist tells us we praise Him for we are "fearfully and wonderfully made" (Ps. 139:14 NKJV). We are His marvelous work. So as cornerstone people who show forth great praises of our Lord, may I just quote the comic Billy Crystal in saying, "you look marvelous" in doing so.

So go forth and shout and shine bright for Him my brothers and sisters of the cornerstone people. Let His glory reign in your hearts. In Jesus's name.

THOUGHTS

PRAYER

DAY 15

"Don't get upset about evil people. Don't be jealous of those
who do wrong. They are like grass and other green plants that dry
up quickly and then die. So trust in the LORD and do good.
Live on your land and be dependable. Enjoy serving the LORD,
and he will give you whatever you ask for. Depend on
the LORD. Trust in him and he will help you"

—Psalm 37:1–5 (ERV)

TRUST, ENJOY, AND *depend* are the key words. Another
translation states trust, delight, and commit. Three actions of the
heart and mind that do well for the believer in trying and tumultuous times. As I meditate on this verse troubles abound in the
world. Political turmoil, global unrest, immorality and corruption seemingly everywhere. And yet God is good. He is still on
the throne, He sees it all, and He is in control. David reminds us
in our passage that evildoers should not upset us. Their day with
the Lord will come, and their evil will be exposed, and their end
will come. Rather than being upset we are to *trust* in the Lord.
Jesus spoke to the disciples of His pending ascension, saying,
"These things I have spoken unto you, that in Me you might have
peace. In the world you shall have trouble; but take heart! I have
overcome the world" (John 16:33 NKJV). Such words of comfort
and strength to live by. All trouble, trials, and tribulations in the
world are turned to joy because the believer has the end result.
Jesus has conquered sin and death giving us victory over the
world. We trust in what God has already done for us. So trust
and continue to do well as unto the Lord, not hiding away, and
the Lord will take care of you.

In such trust, we are also to enjoy, delight, in doing good.
We are to continue and constantly fight the good fight of faith,
enjoying it all in the promise of victory. Attitudes of defeat,

self-loathing, and self-pity will never bring us into a place of peace and rest in our relationship with God. But with attitudes of joy in doing our service in life as Christians we will get answers to prayers and praises for the life of grace and mercy we have.

Finally, we are exhorted to depend on the Lord. We are to commit our ways to the Lord. It's not about us, our abilities, our wants and desires, rights, or happiness. It's about surrender and sacrifice to the Lord's way for our lives. There is an old phrase "let go and let God." It is much better to give God control of our lives and direct our paths. Such is the way of "all things work together for good to those who love God, to those who are called according to His purpose" (Rom. 8:28 NKJV).

Beloved friends, whatever your circumstance, in whatever part of the world you reside, don't be upset or angry. Rather *trust* in Him and His ways. *Enjoy* the ride serving God and doing well, and *depend* on Him to lead the way and direct your path. May the Lord immerse you in much peace and rest as we wait up Him.

THOUGHTS

PRAYER

DAY 16

"The LORD came and stood there. He called as He did before, saying, 'Samuel, Samuel!' Samuel said, 'Speak, I am your servant, and I am listening.'"

—1 Samuel 3:10 (ERV)

TWICE BEFORE DURING the night the Lord had called out Samuel's name. Both times Samuel thought it was Eli calling out, and he rose to answer Eli. He only ended up waking Eli from his sleep until Eli told Samuel it is the Lord calling. Scripture tells us Samuel did not know the Lord because the Lord had not spoken directly to him before. Many commentators believe the calling told here is a physical manifestation of the Lord appearing before Samuel. Samuel, who probably was around twelve years old at the time, hears and receives the direct call to serve from the Lord. It is a beautiful picture of when one dies to self and surrenders their heart to God and is born again. We are in essence responding as a new creation in Christ ready and at His service.

Our passage teaches us that to be a true servant of God there must be a willingness and an availability to serve. Samuel was available to be used. "Speak . . . I am listening." Here I am, Lord, at your service and ready to be your instrument as you see fit. In our service to God, it is not about abilities—God does the equipping for the need (see Moses). It is about availability. In service to God, we must be willing to do anything the Lord asks. Service will be thrust upon us. The needs may pile up one after another and at times on top of each other. We must be available to accept whatever comes our way and without murmuring or complaining, or appeal. And our motive should never be for thanks and pats on the back. This will only lead to self-pity and bitterness when they don't happen. A great example of availability is seen when the prophet Isaiah saw the Lord sitting on the throne in all His glory. He heard the voice of the Lord say, "Who shall I send, and who will go for us?" And Isaiah said, "Here I am! Send me" (Isa. 6:8 ESV). That is availability.

Along with availability, the true servant of God must also be surrendered to God. Samuel answers the Lord saying, "Speak for your servant hears you" (1 Sam. 3:10 ESV). God's servant was waiting for instructions, willing to do what he was told and required to do. Such is the standard of obedience that comes only by way of surrender. And Christian obedience can only come by way of surrender to the cross. Jesus Himself surrendered and became lowly even unto death on the cross for us. Christian service only reaches the heavenly heights of power, authority, and fruit bearing by way of the cross and surrender. Before Isaiah could rightly respond, he too came to the rightful place of surrender when seeing the Lord in all His glory he could only say, "woe is me! For I am undone; because I am a man of unclean lips, and I dwell in the midst of a people of unclean lips; for my eyes have seen the King, the Lord of hosts" (Is. 6:5 KJV).

Our eyes have seen the King on the cross. And the true servant of God knows and surrenders to the King on the cross. It is the place of our utmost humility and selflessness where we are undone and available in service to God. I leave you with these words spoken by Charles Spurgeon: "As long as there is breath in our bodies, let us serve Christ. As long as we can think, as long as we can speak, as long as we can work, let us serve him. Let us serve him with our last gasp."

Oh, Lord that we may be Your surrendered and available servants. For such a time as this, ready to do Your will, Your way. In Jesus's name. Amen.

THOUGHTS

_____

_____

_____

_____

_____

_____

PRAYER

_____

_____

_____

_____

_____

_____

DAY 17

"The Lord said, 'I am the same God your ancestors had—the God of Abraham, the God of Isaac, and the God of Jacob.' Moses began to shake with fear. He was afraid to look at the bush."

—Acts 7:32 (ERV)

IN OUR PASSAGE Dr. Luke is quoting from Exodus 3:6 when the Lord appeared and spoke to Moses on Mt. Sinai in the form of the burning bush and all His glory. It was in the presence of God that Moses body shook, and he was so overwhelmed he could not look. Other Bible versions interpret Moses shaking as trembling. The idea is that Moses was in such total awe and reverence of the Lord's presence that it completely overwhelmed him mentally and physically.

When was the last time you shook or trembled in reverence of God? Is it not true that in our relationship with God we tend to go on with our daily lives, a prayer here, a prayer there, some reading of the Word, going to church (in person or online). It's all good for the heart and soul, but when was the last time you stopped and paused to recognize and revere the awesome presence and work of God in your life?

For some, partaking in communion may be the trigger that brings such a moment. Shaking and trembling may happen at times in our service to God or it may be in those quiet times set aside to be in the presence of God. I have this plaque on the wall in my office that reads "Life is not measured by the number of breaths we take, but by the moments that take our breath away." I love this quote because it speaks to the mind-blowing experiences I have had in the knowledge, reverence, and service of God.

What makes you shake and tremble in the presence of God? Whatever gets you to that place I suggest you find it and engage in it, now more than ever as we see the day approaching. Is it reading in the word about God's glorious creation of the heavens and stars, mountains and oceans, the fowls of the air, and fish of the sea, animals of the earth. Is it when you think about how when God created all of that and said it was good He was thinking of you. That makes me shake and tremble.

Knowing God gave humans free will to love Him and others and provided a plan of redemption to restore our relationship with Him through Jesus Christ who died on the cross and paid the penalty for our sin, that blows my mind. And so does thinking about that glorious morning when Christ rose from the dead, giving us victory over death now and forever more! How about times in the presence and service of God when people are healed, delivered from sin, and those who come to the saving knowledge and grace of the Lord in your presence! Or just the simple awareness and knowledge that Jesus loves you, for the Bible tells you so. When I truly meditate on these things it takes my breath away.

Oh, Lord, let me continue to shake and tremble as I know You and am in Your presence. I cherish these moments that take my breath away, and though they may not be as often as I desire, may my heart always be willing to be aware of Your grace and give You Lord God, the same God as our ancestors, Abraham, Isaac, and Jacob all praise.

THOUGHTS

_____

_____

_____

_____

_____

_____

_____

PRAYER

_____

_____

_____

_____

_____

_____

_____

DAY 18

"Their inheritance by lot, as the LORD had commanded by the hand of Moses, for the nine tribes and the half-tribe."

—Joshua 14:2 (NKJV)

THE BIBLE TELLS us the battle is won. We walk in our Lord's victory. God's promises are real and sure, but there is still work to be done in taking and possessing those promises. The dividing of the promised land in Canaan came by way of casting lots—the trusted and sure Old Testament practice of God's leading. Such practice also testified of God's faithfulness as the lots fell as He had directed.

Today, we don't cast lots as believers. We don't pull out those Magic 8 Balls. We don't roll the dice, 'seek fortune tellers, or set out fleeces before God. Rather, we cast our hearts before the Lord Jesus and trust God's leading and guiding. As the psalmist declares: "Cause me to hear thy lovingkindness in the morning; for in thee do I trust: cause me to know the way wherein I should walk; for I lift up my soul onto thee" (Ps. 143:8 KJV). Believers in the Lord devote and submit their lives to their loving and sovereign God. It is because of this trust, we should accept as Christians whatever lot the Lord God has cast for us. Whether it be a dessert or waterfall, beach or forest, whatever our lot we must treasure it because it comes from God.

King David proclaims, "The LORD is the portion of mine inheritance and of my cup; thou maintainest my lot" (Ps. 16:5 KJV). The apostle Paul tells us "we are his workmanship, created in Christ Jesus unto good works, which God hath before ordained that we should walk in them" (Eph. 2:10 KJV).

We must take and possess our lots in life. Let God lead and do everything as unto His Glory. Our spiritual joy and maturity hinges on it. And as the wonderful hymn by Horatio Spafford reminds us: "whatever my lot, thou hast taught me to say, 'It is well, it is well with my soul.'"

THOUGHTS

_____

_____

_____

_____

_____

_____

PRAYER

_____

_____

_____

_____

_____

_____

DAY 19

"My purpose in telling you to do this is to promote love—the kind of love shown by those whose thoughts are pure, who do what they know is right, and whose faith in God is real."

—1 Timothy 1:5 (ERV)

PAUL TEACHES TIMOTHY and all disciples of Christ with words of exhortation, encouragement, and instruction on Christlike wisdom and ministry guidance. He begins the letter warning Timothy that the church in Ephesus was being deceived by unsound doctrine. That the disciples there were veering away from the gospel and the words of Jesus and getting caught up in Old Testament fables and old wives' tales, questions on genealogies, and putting believers under the bondage of the law.

Our passage today finds Paul exhorting Timothy and the church to get back on track and remember the true message of the gospel, which is to promote the love of God. As with Paul, this should be the purpose of every disciple of Christ. We promote love, not manmade doctrines and opinions that corrupt and divide believers. In promoting the unconditional love of God, Paul tells us three things.

First, it is a love that is pure. Love that is pure is love that comes from a pure heart. Disciples of Christ should have no hidden agendas, no hypocrisy, and no guile attached to their love and actions. God's love does not manipulate, lord over, appease self, but rather it is love that is unconditional, sacrificial, and other serving. This is God's love to and for us, and it is the pure love we should share with others as His disciples. It is a love that is openly transparent. It is not just an outward manifestation of God's love, but it should be an inward manifestation from a pure heart of who we are in Christ Jesus.

Second, it is a love that is right. It is love of a good conscience. Our conscience is the "internal judge accusing of wrong and approving of right." For the disciple of Jesus, doing what is right in the eyes of the Lord is a basic result of Christian love. Good Godly choices of conscience should prevail in our everyday lives, ministries and relationships. Too much wrong and wrong choices are inflicted on the world today. Paul will warn in 1 Timothy 4 that in the later times some believers will depart from faith turning their hearts over to deceitful and seducing spirits, and doctrines of demons, doing wrong speaking lies as hypocrites, having their conscience seared with a hot iron. To sear is to make something withered or dry. A seared conscience will not be able to discern what is right and what is wrong in the eyes of God.

Third, disciples of Christ are to promote love that is real. True Christian love will manifest itself as faith that is real, a love manifested from a sincere heart and sincere faith. The idea being a genuine faith not fake. I am often amazed and saddened as I hear many politicians and people speak of their Christian faith and not only vote but promote ungodly policies. Christian love must exhibit a faith that is real if we are to be effective disciples for the kingdom of God. And real faith can only come from God not man. It is faith that is born in the heart and shared from the heart to others.

As disciples of Jesus, we must be unrelenting in promoting God's love. In doing so, beloved, be sure to check your heart, to be sure your love is pure and genuine. In the words of Jesus "By this shall all know that you are my disciples, if you have love one to another" (John 13:35 NKJV).

THOUGHTS

_____

_____

_____

_____

_____

_____

PRAYER

_____

_____

_____

_____

_____

_____

DAY 20

"Blessed are they which are persecuted for righteousness' sake:
for theirs is the kingdom of heaven."

—Matthew 5:10 (KJV)

PERSECUTION COMES IN many forms. It can be physical or emotional, personal or corporate, but no matter the form, it's never fun. I know I don't feel blessed when persecution comes. I'm not jumping up and down screaming, yippee! Rather, when I think of persecution, I think of the new recruit who when slapped in the face by the sergeant boldly responds, "Thank you, sir, may I have another?"

I am reminded of this scene because I have come to believe the recruit's response is likened to the attitude Christians should have when persecution comes. Jesus tells us to not resist evil but rather when smacked on the cheek to give them the other side to smack you again (Matt. 5:39). Ouch! Although not a believer, Ghandi read this verse and used it for a nation to be freed from British rule. Martin Luther King Jr. was inspired by this same verse to lead the civil rights movement. Peaceful resistance to persecution is part of the core of the heart of God.

The word *persecuted* in our passage means to pursue in a way of hunting down, harassing, vexing, or oppressing. The idea is repeated acts of persecution toward the righteous, God's people. We don't sign up for persecution, but it is inevitable for the Christian. Paul says, "all who live godly in Christ Jesus shall suffer persecution" (2 Tim. 3:12 KJV). Unfortunately, the pages of history are littered with Christians who rather than persevere in persecution went back to their old nets and old ways of the world. See the testimony of Demas in 2 Timothy 4:10.

There is an enemy at work against the Christian. He wants to destroy and at the very least weaken your faith and your joy, rendering your service and witness useless and ineffective. Therefore, do not be surprised or hurt when persecution comes but rather expect it as evidence you are of the righteous of God and doing the righteous service of God. To the persecuted church in Smyrna, Jesus says to fear not and be faithful even if it means death for there is the reward of the crown of life (Rev. 2:10). The prophet Jeremiah grieved under the constant assault of mocking and ridicule, the whispers behind his back, and he concluded "to go on would be difficult but to not go on with the message that burned inside was impossible" (Jer. 20:9).

We have a message to share and a mission to fulfill. As someone once put it: "if you don't have something in life worth dying for, you have nothing worth living for." So onward Christian soldier, press on toward the high call in your life. Persevere in the storms of persecution for "blessed are they which are persecuted for righteousness' sake: for theirs is the kingdom of heaven."

THOUGHTS

_____

_____

_____

_____

_____

_____

PRAYER

_____

_____

_____

_____

_____

_____

DAY 21

"He must increase, but I must decrease."

—John 3:30 (KJV)

SELF MUST DIE. Prior to the arrest and imprisonment of John the Baptist by Herod, his ministry coincided and at times over-lapped with the ministry of our Lord Jesus Christ. Many scholars believe a heated argument arose between John the Baptist's disci-ples and a Jew about purifying rights. It seems what began as doctrinal differences turned personal, and John's disciples were jealous of the popularity of Jesus ministry. The Baptizer's reply, "A person cannot receive even one thing unless it is given him from heaven" (John 3:27 ESV). In that light there should never be a place for competition or jealousy in doing kingdom work. We must die to ourselves if we are to have effective and blessed walks with the Lord as well as effective ministries. The Baptizer's ministry was to be the forerunner of Christ's ministry. John was the messenger who proclaimed the coming of the Messiah. He was the witness pointing to the true light, Jesus. He understood when we die to ourselves, that is when Christ increases in us.

The message of the world is quite the opposite. It tells us we must be all about promoting self. Looking back over the decades, the entertainment industry is a great reflection of self-promo-tion. In the sixties the popular magazines were *Time*, *Look*, and *Life*. In the seventies and eighties there were *People* and *Us* maga-zines. In the nineties and beyond we have *Self* and *Me* magazines. Presently, we take selfies and promote ourselves through the likes of Facebook, Instagram, X, and TikTok.

To share Jesus as Christians, we must get the attention off us and onto our Lord. Self-esteem and self-promotion are best served when dying to self and continually allowing Jesus to make a home in your heart. There is a beautiful old poem that shares how before being born again one pridefully cried all of self and none of Jesus. Then salvation comes and the cry is some of self and some of Jesus. Over time as one grows in the grace and mercy of God, they say in humility less of self and more of Jesus. And then a time comes after we have persevered in our walk at the highest levels of glory and lowest levels of despair when nothing else matters and the heart cries in victory: *none of self, and all of you, Jesus!*

He must increase; I must decrease. Let that be your prayer this day, and every day.

THOUGHTS

PRAYER

DAY 22

"All the men in the army were sad and angry because their sons and daughters were taken as prisoners. The men were talking about killing David with stones. This upset David very much, but he found strength in the LORD his God."

—1 Samuel 30:6 (ERV)

DAVID HAS COME to a very low place in his life. After years of being on the run from King Saul's relentless pursuit, we find David defeated in spirit, having given up hope in the promises of God. He has let go of the promise that he would be king and that his enemies would be defeated. David's circumstances have gotten the better of his heart as he and his men and families sought refuge and safety in the world rather than the Lord God almighty.

The Christian is being tested in the same way today. The world and its ways endlessly pursue our hearts, tempting us with corruption, immorality, wickedness, and persecution'. Sadly, many Christians have gone the way of David, compromising their faith or staying silent to survive and prosper in a world that goes against the truths and promises of God. The true believer will always be convicted and brought back to realize the only thing that matters is to be in the will and purpose of God. Having been expelled by Saul, David and his men backslid and committed atrocities of thievery and even killing the women and children of their enemies. The consequence of such acts forced them to seek refuge in the world trying to join the Philistine army and returning to this place of false security (Ziklag), they discovered their women and children had been taken captive by the same enemies they committed their horrific acts against. David's heart was at rock bottom. His men turned against him even conspiring to stone him to death. The only place he could turn was back to

God. Repenting, David turned his heart to what he knew: the promises and truths of the Lord God almighty. In doing so he found encouragement and strength as the restoring process with God took hold in his heart, and he began afresh and anew in his relationship with God.

Beloved in Christ, we don't have to fall in sin or backslide on our way to rock bottom before God can restore and fill us afresh with a renewed encouragement and strength through the power of the Holy Spirit. The better way is to stay in relationship with God not substituting the comforts the world has to offer. Continually seek God's grace and mercies, compassion, blessings, and leadings in your life. Even in the midst of heavy lamenting of his heart, the prophet Isaiah declared "Through the LORD's mercies we are not consumed, because His compassions fail not. They are new every morning; great is Your faithfulness. 'The LORD is my portion,' says the soul, 'therefore will I hope in Him!'" (Lam. 3:21–24 NKJV).

May our God of mercy, compassion, and truth grant you encouragement and strength, hope and joy this day as you seek and remain in the relentless pursuit of the love God has for you. In Jesus's name. Amen.

THOUGHTS

_____

_____

_____

_____

_____

_____

PRAYER

_____

_____

_____

_____

_____

_____

DAY 23

"Samson told her; 'if they tie me up with seven fresh bowstrings that have not been dried, I will become weak and be like any other man.'"

—Judges 16:7 (HCSB)

THE TESTIMONY OF Samson is that of great tragedy that ends in glorious redemption. It is one where sin abounded much, but grace did much more abound (Rom. 5:20). Samson was consecrated, set apart to and for God, but he lacked in reverent communion with God. He knew God's ways but chose not to engage in the ways of God. He was a man of tremendous godly authority but no accountability. He was a man blessed with great gifts but no greatness. He judged Israel for twenty years but failed to finish the job of delivering the people from the oppression of the Philistines. Instead, Samson slipped into a life of selfish pride that led to a destructive end as he fell in love with the Philistine woman Delilah. Delilah's name means to "impoverish" or "weaken." That is appropriate as Samson, in his spiritual impoverishment, foolishly divulges the key to losing his strength and power and even confesses to Delilah that in losing such he becomes just "like any other man."

Beloved of God, is that what you want for your life? To live outside God's power and strength. Tragically, like Samson, many Christians are living outside the power, purposes, and ways of God just like the people in the world, going through life lacking godly wisdom and power to be their best. Samson knew he was special in the presence and power of God. As a believer, you too are special to and for God. Deut. 7:6 says you "are a holy people to the LORD your God; the LORD your God has chosen you to be a people for Himself, a special treasure above all people on the face of the earth" (NKJV).

The believers fellowship, conversation, power, and very being is to be lovers of God and followers of Christ. This is our reverent communion for a healthy relationship with Him. Without such we are just as any other person of the world being tossed to and fro by worldly ways. Samson knew he was special, and he knew why. Still he forsook his special relationship with God for the pleasures of the world. He was redeemed in his last moments of life. His poor choices used for good. But what could have been? For us, we don't need a testimony of what could have been. Instead, one can chose today to live as the special person you are in Christ. Live to "deny ungodliness and worldly lusts. We should "live soberly, righteously, and godly in this present age, looking for the blessed hope and glorious appearing of the great God and Savior Jesus Christ, who gave Himself for us, that He might redeem us from every lawless deed and purify for Himself *His* own special people, zealous for good works" (Titus 2:12–14 NKJV). We are not to be like others in the world but to be like Christ.

THOUGHTS

_____

_____

_____

_____

_____

_____

PRAYER

_____

_____

_____

_____

_____

_____

DAY 24

"Then all three groups of Gideon's men blew their trumpets
and smashed their jars, The men held the torches in
their left hands and the trumpets in their right hands.
As they blew their trumpets, they shouted, 'A sword
for the LORD and a sword for Gideon.'"

—Judges 7:20 (ERV)

GIDEON AND HIS army of 32,000 men were looking at going to battle against 135,000 of God's enemies, the Midianite army. They were hot and thirsty and filled with anxiety. Many were quite literally "freaking out" as God ordered 22,000 of the men to go home, leaving only 10,000 to fight. One soldier for every 13.5 Midianites. As if that weren't enough, God then separated 300 men from the 10,000 to take on the Midianites. Three hundred against 135,000. Not good odds, and yet God asked for complete obedience and trust for His plan of victory. I doubt Gideon got much sleep the night before the battle, but the Lord managed to give him some sleep because he had a reassuring dream that victory would happen. We are told that after hearing an interpretation of the dream, Gideon worshiped the Lord and in complete obedience and confidence he and his 300 men did exactly as the Lord instructed and defeated the Midianites (Judg. 7:14–25).

The account of this battle and the sounding of the trumpets is a reminder for God's people that to stand against the enemies of God, we must be willing to accept the challenges God allows and be willing to make a great noise when called on by God. To be heard and not silenced. God's people must be willing to ignite fires of faith among God's people to defeat the devil and his ways on earth. What is our great noise? What is our trumpet blast as Christians? We are to proudly (2 Cor. 10:17) and if need be, loudly proclaim the everlasting gospel, the Lord's trumpet, and hold forth the truth of God's light, the Lord's torch.

Who will stand and shout for the Lord today? Who will be obedient to His gospel and truth no matter the odds? Let it be me, and let it be you, beloved in Christ.

THOUGHTS

_____

_____

_____

_____

_____

_____

PRAYER

_____

_____

_____

_____

_____

_____

DAY 25

"I say this because you know that we live in an important time.
Yes, it is now time for you to wake up from your sleep.
Our salvation is nearer now than when we first believed."

—Romans 13:11 (ERV)

WHAT AN AMAZING exhortation. As Paul concludes his instructions on relationships it's as if he pulls out a bullhorn and shouts to the Christian that the days are too short to be wasting time in the nonsense of the world, rather it is high time to be worshipping and serving God!

Paul is saying it is time to *look up, clean up,* and *grow up.* Verse 11 clearly speaks to the second coming of the Lord being near and at hand. As we see the headlines today, this glorious event seems more imminent than ever before, and the last thing we want to be as a believer is found slumbering spiritually. We are to wake up as believers and walk with God everyday spiritually as we navigate the turbulent waters of life. Paul goes on to tell us to also put off works of darkness. As the day approaches, we are to clean up as Christians. We are to live holy lives worshipping the Lord in honesty, decency, and integrity. We are to live our lives for Jesus in worship and truth. The exhortation Paul provides in verse 14 is to grow up. As true followers of Christ whose purpose is to live holy lives as His representatives yielding and being conformed to the image of Christ in all that we do, we are committed to progressing in spiritual maturity. To grow continually "in the grace and knowledge of our Lord" (2 Pet. 3:18 ESV), moving from milk to the meat of God's Word (Heb. 5:13–14), being grounded in our faith through an intimate relationship with the Word of God. The mature Christian makes it their practice to feed the spirit not the flesh, to stay true to word, prayer, and fellowship and revering communion (Acts 2:42).

Mature Christians are committed to growing in their relationship with Christ, walking each day in His victory and not in the devil's defeat.

So beloved, as His people who see and feel the day approaching, may we continue to be awake and may we strive every day to grow in the Lord, cleansing ourselves as we walk in the light and not darkness, and as grown-ups in Christ, let us not grow weary of doing good (2 Thess. 3:13).

THOUGHTS

PRAYER

DAY 26

"Saul sent David away and made him commander over 1000
soldiers. This put David out among the men even more
as they went into battle and returned."

—1 Samuel 18:13 (ERV)

OUR HISTORICAL RECORD shows David being demoted
from essentially being general over all of Saul's army to a
captain of just one thousand soldiers. Saul's jealousy and envy
over David's popularity among the people is leading him to get
David killed or shamed by losing a battle to the people's enemy.
This is an unrealized expectation David is facing in his life, and
yet he does not object or fight Saul's plot against him. Rather,
David continues to behave wisely, staying honorable and faithful
to God's leading in his life, and in doing so the favor of God
continues to be with David.

Sometimes life may not unfold as one expects. Unrealized
expectations can lead one to question God's infinite and sovereign love, wisdom, and leading. Unrealized expectations led
John the Baptist to question if Jesus was the Messiah. Unrealized
expectations led Judas Iscariot to betray our Lord. Unrealized
expectations led Paul to question his own calling and ministry
as he stared down death in a prison cell (Acts 23). And here
David begins a journey he did not expect as Saul will soon start
pursuing David to kill him, which will last for many years. David
will run for his life and often question God, but in the end his
faith and his heart prevail in victory. During the years of persecution, David carried on as a godly man with godly integrity
and godly purpose. He had failures and sin, but He uttered no
bad words about Saul. He never plotted against Saul even when
having an unobstructed opportunity to kill him (1 Sam. 26). He
behaved wisely and found favor with God.

The Lord God has created you and I for the valleys of ordinary things in life not for a life of constant mountain-top experiences. We must accept as believers that life will be full of unrealized expectations. But like David we must continue in faith, behaving wisely so as not to be consumed with chasing or regretting unrealized expectations. Quoting the prophet Isaiah Jesus reminds us that God promises "a bruised reed He will not break, and smoking flax He will not quench" (Matt. 12:20 NKJV), and David tells us "to you, O my Strength, will I sing praises; for God is my defense, my God of mercy" (Ps. 59:17 NKJV), and "For the LORD God is a sun and a shield; the LORD will give grace and glory; no good thing will He withhold from those who walk uprightly" (Ps. 84:11 NKJV).

LORD God, thank you for the lessons of unrealized expectations and the victories over them. Help us to continue to face them wisely all the days of our lives. In Jesus's name. Amen.

THOUGHTS

_____

_____

_____

_____

_____

_____

PRAYER

_____

_____

_____

_____

_____

_____

DAY 27

"Be willing to serve each other out of respect for Christ . . .
a man will leave his father and mother and join his wife,
and the two people will become one."

—Ephesians 5:21 & 31 (ERV)

GOD'S DESIGN FOR husband and wife is to be as one and in harmony with each other. They are to be a compliment to each other. People see a good marriage and they see the couple as one bonded together. The apostle Paul provides a beautiful exhortation for love and God's design for a good marriage in his letter to the Ephesians. The overriding theme is sacrifice and serving one to another.

True sacrifice and service in any relationship begins with God. In the words of Jesus: "Not My will, but Yours, be done" (Luke 22:42 NKJV). "If anyone desires to come after Me, let him deny himself, and take up his cross and follow Me" (Matt. 16:24 NKJV). Lovingly sacrificing and serving in a healthy marriage relationship is the outward extension of one's own submission to Christ. It's quite the opposite of the world we live in where relationships often reflect lives of selfies and self-promotion. But as the apostle Paul teaches us, it is in submission to Christ that pride is replaced by humility, and self is replaced by sacrifice and service.

A Christ-like marriage will reflect the love of Jesus as exemplified in His love for the church—a love that is divine and supernatural. A sacrificial love that is unconditional and unwavering. A love that serves one another. Christ's love is the scarlet thread that runs through healthy marriages. And when the love of Christ is the center of a marriage, it creates a bond that is not easily broken as two are one. The writer of Ecclesiastes tells us "two are better than one because they have a good reward for their efforts. For if either falls, 'his companion can lift him up; but pity the one who falls without another to lift him up. . . . And if someone overpowers one person, two can resist him. A cord of three strands is not easily broken" (Eccl. 4:9–13 CSB).

In God's divine wisdom, He shows us through Christ that the love of sacrifice and service to each other is the key to a good marriage. It is His perfect wisdom that can work in a marriage. For we know as the husband lovingly sacrifices and serves his wife, so the wife in turn will lovingly sacrifice and serve her husband. And as the husband loves more, the wife responds in love more. And as the wife loves more, the husband will be apt to love more, and on and on love goes, an endless love and bond for one another like the rings on their fingers—the perfect circle of God's love intended for perfect marital harmony. Me, she, and Jesus. That is the strength of my marriage. The more of Jesus and the less of me leads to more happiness and joy for she and me.

THOUGHTS

PRAYER

DAY 28

*"But there were false prophets also among the people, even as
there shall be false teachers among you, who privily (in secret)
shall bring in damnable heresies, even denying the Lord that
bought them and bring upon themselves swift destruction."*

—2 Peter 2:1 (KJV)

THE APOSTLE PETER is warning against false prophets and
teachers among those in the church who deny the deity of Jesus
Christ and His blood atonement. The apostle Paul also warned
after his departing "savage wolves [or extortioners] will come in
among you, not sparing the flock. Also from among yourselves
men will rise up, speaking perverse things to draw away disciples
after themselves" (Acts 20:29–30 NKJV).

From the beginning of the church age the devil quickly
learned that he could not beat the church and God's people from
outside attacks, so it was best to join them and create his havoc
from the inside. We see the evidence of this work in Ananias
and Sapphira deceiving the early church in Jerusalem (Acts 5).
It is also seen in the early church legalists subverting church
souls with the misleading and condemnation of their hearts.
Peter himself, under the influence of Satan, tried to lead Jesus
down a deceptive path and was rebuked for it by the Lord (Matt.
16:21–23). Paul tells us "a little leaven leaveneth the whole lump"
(Gal. 5:9 KJV). False teaching is equated to yeast as just a little
bit grows quickly, permeating completely. The goal is to seduce
hearts and get them to move away from truth saying, "follow me
and my way rather than following Jesus and His way."

It is interesting that Peter also tells us the false teachers are not
our problem as their day of judgment will come and no defense
will be accepted, and their destruction will be swift. Peter reminds
the believer that whatsoever one sows they will reap (Gal. 6:7).

Jude speaks of such as the ungodly who come into the church by stealth, turning God's grace into lewd and fleshly desires as they are brute beasts who corrupt themselves (v.4). They are like animals without God-given human reasoning.

Beloved in Christ, in a world where falseness is all around us, and where falsities seem ever present in the church, our hope and strength are in the trusted Word of God. The devil wants to sift us like wheat so the weak in spirit can fall. But as Jesus prayed for Peter, He is praying for us that our faith never fails. As we confront lies, heresies, hypocrisies, and the many winds of doctrine blowing through the church, remember to "not believe every spirit, but test the spirits, whether they are of God; because many false prophets have gone out into the world" (1 John 4:1 NKJV). Keep your eyes and hearts on Jesus and the Word, and you will see and hear through all the fog and noises of deception and corruption in this world. For it is on Christ the solid rock we stand. All other ground is sinking sand.

THOUGHTS

_____

_____

_____

_____

_____

_____

_____

PRAYER

_____

_____

_____

_____

_____

_____

DAY 29

"Pray at all times in the Spirit with every prayer and request, and stay alert with all perseverance and intercession for all the saints."

—Ephesians 6:18 (HCSB)

IN HIS LETTER to the church in Ephesus the apostle Paul emphasizes unity for as believers we are all one in Christ. He speaks to the church and God's people about their obligations to live set apart from the world as Christians, and he warns about warfare that will come against Christians who are living for God. The warfare he writes about is beyond the natural temptations of the flesh but is spiritual and with powers that are unseen yet real. Without Christ the believer is powerless against them. But we have the spiritual armor of God—the defensive weapons of truth, righteousness, peace, faith, and salvation and the offensive weapons of the Word of God and prayer to counterattack the fiery darts of the enemy. Prayer is mentioned last' because it is our most powerful resource against spiritual warfare. As a wise person once said: "you can do more after you have prayed, but you can do nothing before you pray."

In our passage Paul offers up four characteristics of prayer. The first is to pray at all times. Prayer is to be of the utmost priority and a constant activity in our lives. As the theologian Warren Wiersbe wrote: "A Christian must 'pray always' because he is always subject to temptations and attacks of the devil. A surprise attack has defeated more than one believer who forgot to 'pray without ceasing'" (*The Wiersbe Bible Commentary: New Testament*, David C. Cook, 2007, 624). Secondly, Paul tells us our prayers are to be anointed. We are to pray at all times in the Spirit. Now, I don't always feel like praying. However, I have learned to pray even when I don't feel like it. I pray, wait, and keep praying with intent to be spiritually led in my prayers. In time, my attitude and spirit bring anointed prayers. Third, Paul says to pray with perseverance. Believers are to keep praying even when we have no answers to prayer. You may remember the poster of a cat hanging by its front paws from a bar with the caption that read: "Hang in there, Baby!" Sometimes that's a picture of exactly what we have to do as Christians in our prayers. Answers don't always come quickly, so we must not give up praying. Fourthly, Paul shares that prayer is to include intercession. As Christians we are called to pray for one another. Sharing in the Spirit each other's burdens through prayer. We are to also pray for those outside the grace of God, and we pray for our enemies (Matt. 5:44).

So beloved in Christ, pray always in the Spirit of God, persevering and interceding on behalf of others. Pray that God would move mountains as well as those pesky little ant hills. Prayer can bind Satan and his demons from influencing territories. Prayer can break the chains of bondage Satan has a hold on people. Prayer can change and effect the hearts of world leaders. Prayer can cut through and destroy the evil permeating so much of society and culture. *But we must pray!* It is our duty as the righteous of God to pray for "the effective, fervent prayer of a righteous man avails much" (James 5:16 NKJV).

THOUGHTS

PRAYER

DAY 30

"Therefore, I want the men in every place to pray,
lifting up holy hands without anger or argument."

—1 Timothy 2:8 (CSB)

IN HIS EXHORTATION to Timothy, Paul tells God's people to pray for everyone (1 Tim. 2:1). Praying for kings and those in authority will benefit the believer in the ability to lead quiet and peaceable lives. He then shares his own prayer in wanting men to take the lead in praying everywhere lifting up holy hands. The culture of the Old Testament often depicts worship and prayer with the lifting of hands in the air and is the practice of many believers today. We must take notice that Paul is emphasizing in the lifting of hands to make sure they are holy. The prophet Isaiah spoke of how God said to the people, "Even though you make many prayers, I will not hear. Your hands are full of blood" (Isa. 1:15 NKJV). They had sinned against God, there was no repentance, and thus their hands were unholy, and their devotion was a hypocrisy to God.

When we worship, when we pray, regardless of posture, we are to come before the throne of God washed and cleansed of sin or seeking such a washing and cleansing with confession, receiving a fresh filling of our Lord's mercy and grace and forgiveness. This is what holy hands look like. And Paul emphasizes that we are to be free of anger and arguments within our relationships in life when presenting our worship and prayers to God. What that means is our hearts are to be pure before God. We are not to harbor wrath or bad feelings toward another. We are not to be disputing among ourselves. Ideally, we are to reconcile our differences with one another (Matt. 5:23–24). And in our prayer life we are to pray *to* God not *at* Him, and we pray *with* others not preaching *to* them in our prayers.

THOUGHTS

PRAYER

DAY 31

*"But even if God does not save us, we want you to know,
King, that we refuse to serve your gods. We will not
worship the gold idol you have set up."*

—Daniel 3:18 (ERV)

WHENEVER I READ this passage my heart bursts with joy as it is possibly the greatest proclamation of faith in the Bible. Shadrach, Meshach, and Abednigo refused to worship the ninety-foot-tall golden idol that King Nebuchadnezzar had erected and commanded everyone to worship. The king was angry and demanded they bow down, and this was their reply. The king then orders the furnace to be turned up to seven times hotter than usual, and the three young men were thrown into the fire. But suddenly there was a fourth who joined them in the fire. It was our Lord, our Deliverer and Savior, and Shadrach, Meshach and Abednigo came forth from the fire with not a burn on their bodies, not a hair even singed, and their robes fully intact. Nebuchadnezzar was stunned and the Scripture says in that moment he believed and ordered all the people to praise and worship the God of Shadrach, Meshach, and Abednigo. A great proclamation of faith followed by a great deliverance from the fire turned into a great scene of worship.

A believer's sincere and earnest worship of God will always be formed and forged by our faith and obedience to God. For Shadrach, Meshach, and Abednigo this proclamation of their great faith began when King Nebuchadnezzar laid seize to Jerusalem in 605 BC, pillaged the temple treasures, and took hundreds of Israelites captive, including Daniel and these three young men (Dan. 1). They were children of rulers, likened to West Point graduates, the cream of the crop, all in their early teens. They were taken hostage to be indoctrinated in Babylon's heinous ways, and to keep Israel's rulers in check with the threat of harming their children. But when the time came to partake in Babylonian pleasures and fine dining, these young men "purposed in [their] hearts" to not defile themselves by eating the king's delicacies (Dan. 1:8 NKJV). The word *purpose* in the Hebrew means to "thoughtfully observe and compile all the information." In other words, from a faith already formed and forged in worship and praise and practice, Daniel and his friends, when tempted with the Babylonian pleasures, observed the worldly gods that were being worshiped, the pleasures being offered, and they reasoned it did not add up with what they knew to be true and worthy. Much of it was an offense to the true God. So they purposed in their hearts—a steadfast choice—not to defile, nor pollute nor stain themselves before their God.

The heart is where the battle of faith is forged and played out and will determine the true heart of one's worship to God. Proverbs tells us to "keep [guard] our hearts with all diligence; for out of it are the issues of life" (Pro. 4:23 NKJV). A purposed heart is a surrendered heart. A surrendered heart results in a faithful and obedient life, producing a worship to God that is real and everlasting. Friend, how real and sincere is your worship to God? Even if God does not heal you, provide for your finances, bring a spouse to you, draw back your prodigal or prodigals, will you still refuse to bow to the world and continue to worship the one and true God and our Lord Jesus Christ?

Even if God does not, choose to continue to worship the Lord God and Him alone. To worship you Oh King, and Oh Lord!

THOUGHTS

_____

_____

_____

_____

_____

PRAYER

_____

_____

_____

_____

_____

DAY 32

"Casting all your cares upon Him, for He cares for you."

—1 Peter 5:7 (NKJV)

AS A CHILD of God your relationship with the heavenly Father should be secure in knowing that He cares for you. The Bible is unwavering in proclaiming that God cares for your needs (Jehovah-Jireh), your afflictions (Jehovah-Rapha), your welfare and well-being (Jehovah-Rohi). He is the all-sufficient source of our blessings, and no problem is too big for God to handle (El Shaddai). To know such truths is to trust in God. To trust in God means we must surrender and cast our cares upon Him to deal with them. We are not to ignore our cares, but rather to give them over to the Lord God for His wisdom, His leading, and ultimately His solutions.

The word *cast* in the Greek that Peter used means literally "to throw." Peter's letter is written with the theme of hope to the believer in the context of persecution, which they were suffering. At times, our problems and issues in life can be so overwhelming that we must throw them upon the Lord. It's as if they come upon us like a live grenade. Don't hang on but throw it away. As a student of the Scriptures, Peter no doubt was thinking of David who in lamenting before God about the oppression and wickedness coming against him, testifies of our Lord's care: "Cast thy burden upon the LORD, and he shall sustain thee. He shall never suffer the righteous to be moved" (Ps. 55:22). The word *cast* in the Hebrew that David used means "to let go." David was speaking to problems and issues of life but not in the state of being overwhelmed. Rather, David suggests that problems will come and go so just relax and let go of the burden you carry and give it to the Lord for He cares for you. Jesus Himself declares: "Come to Me, all *you* who labor and are heavy laden, and I will give you rest.

Take My yoke upon you and learn from Me, for I am gentle and lowly in heart, and you will find rest for your souls. For My yoke *is* easy and My burden is light." (Matt. 11:28–30 NKJV).

Whatever issues you are dealing with know and trust that God cares for you and wants to help you. Whether you need to hand your troubles to the Lord or throw them like a grenade that is about to go off, give it to God. Jesus Himself testified of the wonderful care that God has for us in the garden of Gethsemane the night of His arrest. Knowing the burden of taking the place of judgment for all the sins of mankind—past, present, and future—He pleaded with God, asking if there be any other way to save mankind other than being spiritual separated from the Father to please let that happen! However, in submission, Jesus's heart cried out, "nevertheless, not as I will, but as You will" (Matt. 26:39).

Are you troubled, burdened, anxious, worried, over a matter? Father knows best. Let go and let God. Cast your burden upon Him because He greatly cares for you.

THOUGHTS

PRAYER

DAY 33

"...serving the Lord with all humility."

—Acts 20:19 (CSB)

PAUL'S MINISTRY WAS filled with all manners of persecution, trials, and sufferings. He survived shipwrecks, beatings, imprisonment, rocks being thrown at him, the ridicule of people, and yet he continued faithfully in the ministry. How was Paul able to carry on the way he did? The answer is found in our passage; Paul served the Lord and not people. Because of the need to be accepted and satisfy self, many Christians serve people rather than the Lord. In doing so they fail in their service and at times ministry. Burnout, dissatisfaction, bitterness, and weariness set in. It may be a short time; it may be years, but when serving people rather than the Lord, eventually your strength fails. The rejections and bruises will be too much to handle and one will give up on their service, or worse, run from their faith., However, when you step into ministry and service and choose to do it as unto the Lord (Col. 3:23) out of reverence for God and what He has done for you, then the hardships, persecutions, and trials of life will not deter you. Instead, serving will fill you with joy, not the fleeting self-fulfilling emotions of happiness and self-worth.

Paul also reminds us in our passage that true service will be to God, and it will be done in humility. Paul knew the effectiveness of his ministry and gifts. He also knew he was effective by God's grace, and it was not of himself. Such humility leads our service and ministry to the place of esteeming others before oneself (Phil. 2:3). The Greek word for *esteem* means "to consider." Regardless of what you may think, every person you come across in life is more talented, more gifted at something than you. A humble servant of God recognizes this and does not seek to find fault with others, nor judge another, but rather considers them and exalts them in the Lord. Are their problems in your marriage? Esteem your spouse over yourself. Having difficulties with someone at work? Esteem that person before yourself. Do you have issues with your church or people at your church? Esteem them better than yourself.

To serve the Lord with all humility is to deny self and submit to Christ's authority and to walk in obedience to God. True humility will look to the welfare of others as our Lord did on earth. It is to ask what your part is in the work God is doing and to be satisfied with it. Humility dictates we are to be a better person to your fellow brothers and sisters in the Lord and to live as better people in society. To look at people not down on them or over them. Paul says that Jesus humbled Himself even unto death (Phil. 2:8). Beloved, I implore you to read 1 Corinthians 13:5–8 and be as Jesus. Serve Him and only Him in all humility.

THOUGHTS

_____

_____

_____

_____

_____

_____

PRAYER

_____

_____

_____

_____

_____

_____

DAY 34

*"And I pray that you and all God's holy people will have
the power to understand the greatness of Christ's love—how wide,
how long, how high, and how deep that love is."*

—Ephesians 3:18 (ERV)

IN PAUL'S LETTER to the Ephesians he prays for Christians to
be spiritually strengthened through the Holy Spirit so that Christ
may dwell in our hearts through faith in ways beyond our own
doing. It is the knowing of God's love in a divine relationship—a
love that passes human knowledge and understanding. Paul
describes this love of God as being beyond any measurements of
width, length, height, and depth, and it is a love that transcends
all of mankind.

To know this love of God one must be rooted and grounded
in God's love (Eph. 3:17). Our relationship with God fills us with
His love and is a living testimony of our lives. It produces lives that
manifest joy, peace, longsuffering, gentleness, goodness, faith,
and self-control (Gal. 5:22). To know such the love of God and to
live in the richness and fullness of this love, we look no further
than the cross at Calvary. In his letter to the Romans the apostle
Paul declares that "God demonstrates His own love for us in that
while we were still sinners, Christ died for us" (Rom. 5:8 NKJV).

The only way I can truly know and truly understand God's
love for me is at the cross of Calvary. There one can see the width
of God's love with the outstretched hands of Jesus. The cross shows
us the length of His suffering which was even before the foundations of the world (Rev. 13:8). The depth of our God's love is seen
and heard in our Lord's cry from the cross: "My God! My God!
Why have You forsaken me?" (Matt. 27:46). And the height of
God's love is forever seen in Jesus's prayer from the cross: "Father,
forgive them, for they do not know what they do" (Luke 23:34

NKJV) and our Lord's final words from the cross: *Tetelestai*, "It is finished" (John 19:30). The debt paid, love complete.

Do not forsake the importance and impact of the cross on your faith Beloved of God. It is the cross where we are rooted and grounded in God's love for us. We can know that which cannot be humanly understood and be filled with the fulness of God.

THOUGHTS

PRAYER

DAY 35

"But the one who endures to the end will be saved."

—Matthew 24:13 (CSB)

PERSEVERANCE MEANS PERSISTENCE in doing something despite difficulty or delay in achieving success. The actions of perseverance include endurance, patience, and steadfastness. For the Christian perseverance is necessary as we hope for Jesus Christ and His return. I have heard Christian perseverance described as one waiting for a bus at an open-air bus stop in the middle of a hailstorm. This is an accurate visual of a Christian enduring till the end whether it is our Lord's return or the end of our faith journey here on earth.

In our passage Jesus Himself is looking to the end of the ages through the great tribulation when many will be saved but they will have to persevere and endure great persecution and even death. One of the elders around God's throne in heaven asked the apostle John "'who are these people in white robes, and where did they come from?' John replied to him, 'sir, you know.' And the elder said 'these are the ones coming out of the Great Tribulation. They have washed their robes and made them white in the blood of the Lamb'" (Rev. 7:14 NKJV).

Perseverance and enduring are not just for the great tribulation saints. Every Christian in every generation has had to endure, with patience, as faith is always put to the test with various trials, temptations, and sufferings. The psalmist cries out, "You know the insults I endure—my shame and disgrace. You are aware of all my adversaries" (Psalm 69:19 CSB). The apostle Paul declares, "we labor, working with our own hands. When we are reviled, we bless; when we are persecuted, we endure it" (1 Cor. 4:12 CSB). And he continues, "We endure everything so that we will not hinder the gospel of Christ" (1 Cor. 9:12 CSB). That's heavy. We are to persevere so as not to hinder God's message from going forth. But those who endure shall be saved! What a glorious promise to the faithful Christian.

I am inspired by the story of the early twentieth century explorer Ernest Shackleton who with a full crew was the first to set sail across the Antarctic ocean. Their ship getting stuck and then crushed in the shifting ice hundreds of miles from help and with no ability to communicate. They fled to the desolate Elephant Island off the tip of Antarctica. Captain Shackleton and two of his officers set sail in one their lifeboats on a miraculous and heroic mission for help while the crew remained behind on the island enduring four and a half months with no shelter, sub-zero temperatures, and only penguins to eat, thousands of them. But who wants to kill and eat a guy in a tuxedo? Not me. As they persevered in their suffering, the only book they had to read was the Bible as all other paper was used for fire. The crew read from the Bible and had Bible studies every day. They patiently endured clinging to the hope they would be rescued and saved. In the end God prevailed, and Captain Shackleton and his officers brought a ship to save them. Most though chose never to eat fowl again.

In our relationship with the Lord, trials and persecution will come and go but we must endure, we must persevere with patience to the end. Our life as a Christian is an endurance race. Paul tells us to run that we may obtain the prize (1 Cor. 9:24). In Hebrews we are exhorted to put aside the nonsense and minutia of sin which hinders our race and instead run with patience the life that is set before us keeping our eyes and hope on Jesus Christ, the author and finisher of our race of faith who for the joy of your salvation, endured the cross for you (Heb. 12:1–2). We are to endure suffering as a faithful soldier of Jesus Christ (2 Tim. 2:3), and blessed are those who have endured in seeking heavenly things, the Word of God which endures unto everlasting life, not the worldly things that perish (John 6:27).

The race of faith is won with the knowledge and understanding of God's love testified by His Word. It is the hope that enables the Christian to persevere in patience the race knowing God is with you, God is for you, and God loves you, which is why He sent His only begotten son to die for you that in Him you can do all things; you can endure to the end.

THOUGHTS

PRAYER

DAY 36

"These all continued with one accord in prayer and supplication."

—Acts 1:14 (KJV)

THANKSGIVING IS NOT just a day of feast or day of thanks. Thanksgiving is a reminder of the need for gratitude. The attitude of gratitude that should be part of our everyday lives as Christians. In all honesty, though, some days, some seasons we fail to muster up much gratitude for all that God has done in our lives.

Moses had to deal with a whole group of people who failed in their gratitude toward God. It was God who parted the Red Sea for them, who delivered them from the bondage of Egypt, who provided a cloud by day for shade in their dessert journey and a fire by night to light their way. The Lord God made the bitter waters sweet, and provided manna, the bread from heaven for their daily sustenance. Rather than maintaining attitudes of gratitude for all that God had done, the Israelites murmured and complained. They grumbled, "We remember the fish which we ate freely in Egypt, the cucumbers, the melons, the leeks, the onions, and the garlic; ⁶ but now our whole being *is* dried up; *there is* nothing at all except this manna *before* our eyes!'" (Num. 11:5–6 NKJV). It reminds me of the story of a religious zealot who took a vow of silence in which he could utter only two words every five years. After the first five years the zealot appeared before his elders and when asked to speak, he declared, "bad food." Another five years go by and again coming before the elders to speak, he says: "bed hard." Five more years of silence go by, and the zealot appears again before the elders and proclaims, "I quit!" A wise elder looks at the zealot and says, "well, it's no wonder you quit. All you've been doing around here the last fifteen years is complaining!" The zealot had shelter, food, and a bed, but his attitude lacked gratitude. Paul commenting on the Israelites lack of gratitude warns us not to "complain as some of them did. Because they complained, they were killed by the angel that destroys" (1 Cor. 10:10 CSB). God has a way of dealing with unthankful and ungrateful hearts. It is always best to stay in a place of gratitude no matter your situation in life.

In our verse for today, Jesus has gone to heaven leaving the disciples the promise and exhortation to go speak the good news of the gospel. Not understanding, the disciples return to Jerusalem, their Messiah gone, hopes dashed, fearing persecution, and still they gathered together in faith and in purpose, a reflection of gratitude as they wait on the Lord. How many of us, despite our circumstances, wait for the Lord, seeking and praying, or do we crumble and panic, murmur and complain when life does not go the way we want or expect? For the disciples, their gratitude for just the knowledge and love of their Savior ushered in the baptism of the Holy Spirit upon them, and the greatest moment of grace and mercy and truth and power was unleashed on the world that day.

Attitude can cripple or bless you. Job, after losing everything proclaims, "Though He slay me, yet will I trust Him. Even so, I will defend my own ways before Him. He also shall be my salvation" (Job 13:15 NKJV). That's an attitude of gratitude. It turned out well for Job. Beloved, Jesus saved you. He bled and died for you on the cross. He paid your penalty as a sinner, delivering you from the bondage of sin and death to a lively hope of eternal glory. How can you not be thankful for all He has done for you? How can the greatest act of love not muster up attitudes of gratitude in your heart, regardless of circumstances. This day, commit your life to being a celebration of gratitude. Rejoice always and in everything give thanks, for this is the will of God in Christ Jesus concerning you.

THOUGHTS

_____

_____

_____

_____

_____

_____

PRAYER

_____

_____

_____

_____

_____

_____

_____

DAY 37

"My soul, praise the LORD! Every part of me,
praise his holy name."

—Psalm 103:1 (ERV)

PSALM 103 IS the great call to praise the Lord. It is the call to immerse yourself in gratefulness and thanksgiving for all God has done and promises to do in your life. It is testimony of praise in response to knowing that a loving God forgives us of our sins. He heals our diseases, redeems us from destruction, crowns us with love and compassion, satisfies our needs, and metes out righteousness and justice.

The word *praise* in our verse today is sometimes translated as *bless*. It is the Hebrew word *barak*, which means an act of adoration and is derived from the root of the Hebrew word for kneel. King David is speaking to a place of position where we praise and worship God. The place of thanks, thankfulness, and gratitude. It is the attitude of praise from a place of humility that should pour out of our very souls toward God. David is calling us to praise and thank God not just with our voices but with our hearts, minds, and souls, our entire beings.

Thanks, thankfulness, gratitude, are all acts of adoration to the Lord. When Daniel is called on to interpret King Nebuchadnezzar's dream, he understands that the wisdom given to him came from God. His heart cried out, "I thank and praise you, God of my ancestors: You have given me wisdom and power, you have made known to me what we asked of you, you have made known to us the dream of the king" (Dan. 2:23 NIV). Paul, who came under such attack and persecution, was so thankful for fellow Christians and fellowship, he repeatedly expressed adoration (see Rom. 1:8, 1 Cor. 1:4, Eph. 1:16, Phil. 1:3, Col. 1:3, 2 Thess. 1:3; 2:13 and Phil. 4). In Romans 16:3 Paul specifically expresses in adoration how all the gentile churches are thankful for Priscilla and Aquilla who risked their lives for Paul.

So like Daniel and the apostle Paul, praise God today. Worship and adore our Lord with your entire being. Praise Him from a position of humility and gratitude not just for all God does but just for who He is: a loving, kind, compassionate, merciful, wonderful Father who loves you and adores you.

THOUGHTS

PRAYER

DAY 38

"And without controversy great is the mystery of godliness..."

—1 Timothy 3:16 (NKJV)

PAUL'S FIRST PASTORAL letter to Timothy is an exhortation in matters of the church. Timothy cared for the church in Ephesus at the time and was waging spiritual war against false teachings and needed the right message along with qualified godly leaders to rise up within the church and the body of Christ. The words from our passage *without controversy* translates from the Greek to something like "confessedly." It conveys the idea of no deceit, no misunderstanding. What Paul is proclaiming is that gospel godliness has the full authority and agreement from God himself in relationship to Christ and the church—without controversy.

Paul goes on to proclaim that God was manifested in the flesh (without controversy) as God became man in the form of Jesus Christ, and He dwelt among us (John 1:14). The eyewitness accounts of Jesus in the flesh are irrefutable (without controversy). He goes on to declare (without controversy) that Jesus's public ministry began when the Holy Spirit came upon the Lord in the form of a dove (Matt. 3:16). Paul states (without controversy) how Jesus was victorious over the temptations of the devil in the wilderness for forty days and was then ministered to by angels (Matt. 4:11). Jesus preached unto the gentiles (without controversy). Simeon, who would not see death before seeing the Messiah, saw Jesus in the temple with His parents and declared, "For my eyes have seen your salvation . . . a light to bring revelation to the Gentiles and the glory of Your people Israel" (Luke 2:30, 32 NKJV). And Paul also proclaims (without controversy) that Jesus was "believed on in the world." The Roman centurion seeing Jesus on the cross declared, "truly this was the Son of God" (Matt. 27:54 NKJV). Received up into glory (without controversy), Jesus is in heaven where He prays and intercedes for you and me (Heb. 7:25), and He will come again to receive us. "Let not your heart be troubled . . . I go to prepare a place for you." (John 14:1–2 NKJV).

Jesus Christ came to us. He dwelt among us. He lived and died for us, and He lives now in us the believer. That is the mystery of godliness revealed. Fifteen times the word *godliness* is found in the New Testament and eleven of those instances were written by Paul in the pastoral letters to Timothy and Titus, which speaks of the need for true and sincere godliness in the church—without controversy. Life can be overwhelming. We may feel unqualified and ill-equipped to serve in ministry. We may have failed in our right relationship with the Lord. But be encouraged, beloved of God, for in Jesus we need no gurus, no systems, no programs trying to be blameless before God. We just need the person of Jesus living in us through the power of the Holy Spirit. The apostle Peter says it well: "His divine power has given us everything required for life and godliness through the knowledge of Him who called us by His own glory and goodness" (2 Pet. 1:3 CSB).

Without controversy!

THOUGHTS

_____

_____

_____

_____

_____

_____

PRAYER

_____

_____

_____

_____

_____

_____

DAY 39

"And the children of Issachar, which were men that had
understanding of the times, to know what Israel ought to do."

—1 Chronicles 12:32 (KJV)

IN THE BOOK of first Chronicles we are told the testimony of the twelve tribes of Israel and their captains aligning their support and allegiance to David to be king. Their allegiance and loyalties were previously aligned with King Saul, who is now dead, and they refuse to serve Saul's son Abner. The captains understand that now is the time, for such a time as this, to align with David for it was decreed by God that he would be the rightful king (2 Sam. 2:4).

Our passage is so relevant and important for the Christian in today's world perhaps now more than ever in history for we need understanding of the times. As one commentator stated: "the understanding the men in our passage had was that of political sagacity." They had the ability to make good judgments in relationship to the events in the world and their circumstances. They were observers of the state of affairs in life and country and sought to apply godly wisdom to their actions and choices. They rightly discerned the politics, providing them the ability to make good judgment with timely wisdom.

As Christians, we cannot be in the dark with the issues of life. This includes aspects of social and political issues. We need divine understanding from God for the times in which we live. Over and over Jesus rebuked His generation for not discerning the times. Paul admonishes believers to know the times and wake up out of our ignorance, for "our salvation is nearer than when we first believed" (Rom. 13:11 NKJV). And Jeremiah during the time of Israel's exile exhorts God's people to discern their circumstances within the divine and sovereign plan of God and

His unfailing purposes for His people (Jer. 27–29). We live in a society that is past feeling that "has given themselves over unto lasciviousness to work all uncleanness with greediness" (Eph. 4:19 NKJV).

Beloved child of God, our hearts and minds must be like those of the men of Issachar. We need now more than ever to be people who understand the times in which we live and the spiritual attacks and battles that are directly leading the world into the final days. Jesus warns us that "when these things begin to happen, look up and lift up your heads, because your redemption draws near"' (Luke 21:28 NKJV). To understand what's going on around us in all aspects of life, we need to be "look up" people. We need heavenly understanding to judge and make right decisions and actions for us, our loved ones, and the ones we serve and minister to. We need to be strong in spirit and understanding, to be steadfast in our faith, unwavering in our truth, and willing to make a stand for Jesus.

Lord, we need You. We need Your divine understanding for these times. Let us not be found unwise nor ignorant to the schemes of the wicked. Let us be strong in Your love and grace unto the end.

THOUGHTS

PRAYER

DAY 40

"Going a little further, he fell facedown and prayed,
"My Father, if it is possible, let this cup pass from me.
Yet not as I will, but as you will."

—Matthew 26:39 (CSB)

TRUST IS A complicated issue as it relies on the truth, ability, and strength of something or someone. Trust is like a two-edged sword that cuts both ways. It is good, but it can also be devastatingly bad when broken. We trust in things every day: The lights to go on; our car to start; safe passage along roadways, bridges, and through the air. When things fail it is devastating as trust in things and systems are broken. The same happens in our relationships with people. A word not kept, promises broken, actions of betrayal all destroy the bond of trust in a relationship. This is why it is so important to know God will always remain true and trust in Him can never be broken by God. Moses trusted God when it seemed there was no escape from Egypt's pursuing army. King David trusted God in the midst of circumstances not going as expected. Noah trusted God when building the ark year after year with the unending mocking and ridicule. Each of these historical people trusted in God's promises to them, and they believed God's way was best.

In our passage today we read of perhaps the most inspirational example of trust one could have. Jesus, foreseeing the agony and suffering before Him as He is praying, and the greater torment of being spiritually separated from His Father in heaven, cries out: "O My Father, if it is possible, let this cup pass from Me; nevertheless, not as I will, but as You *will.*" (Matt. 26:39 NKJV). Jesus is pleading with God. He asks if there can be any other way to save mankind, any way but by His suffering, death, and separation from the Father. If there is any method, plan, anything at all God, let it be possible.

As a four-year-old boy growing up in Minnesota, my parents wanted me to learn skiing early as my brother and sister had. These were the days of leather lace boots and cable bindings for the skis. On one occasion I was with my mom and was attempting to get on a chair lift for my first time. Sitting back but not far enough, we went up in the air and after about fifteen feet I fell off and landed into a soft pile of snow. As I lay there and the chair kept going with my mom on it looking back at me, I reached out and just started crying for her. I felt an overwhelming feeling of separation in my time of need. She assured me it would be alright. I took the next chair with one of the operators. When I reached the top, I gave my mom perhaps the biggest hug of my entire life.

My minor separation and testing were nothing like what our Lord faced in the garden of Gethsemane. Jesus knew He had to pay the ultimate price for God's way in their love for us. He knew He had to trust the Father. Where is your trust in God today? Or perhaps the deeper question is where is your threshold of trusting in God and His way and plans for your life? Do you allow certain circumstances or perhaps a recent incident to bring distrust and separation into your heart? The Bible says God's ways are perfect and His words are true and flawless (Ps. 18:30). The Bible says God cannot lie (Num. 23:19, Heb. 6:18, Tit. 1:2). Do you trust in God that no matter what you come across in life, it will work for good in the end (Rom. 8:28)? Do you trust that Jesus has gone and prepared a place for you in heaven and will receive you for all eternity (John 14)? Do you trust there are eternal rewards that await you (Matt. 5:12, Luke 6:23, 1 Cor. 3:14, 1 Cor. 9:18–26)? Do you trust (like Jesus did in the garden), that God's plan of salvation for you is through His son Jesus Christ who is the way, the truth, and life (John 14:6)?

Beloved of Christ, in the world trust must be earned, but with God trust is complete and perfect. It's up to you to choose and partake in a trusting relationship with Him. Don't depend on yourself, but rather depend on Him and acknowledge Him and His ways (Prov. 3:5–6). Turn from the wicked ways of the world (2 Tim. 2:22). Listen and guard your heart (2 Tim. 1:14), and trust in God's love and promises as He is with you, until the end (Matt. 28:20).

THOUGHTS

_____

_____

_____

_____

_____

_____

PRAYER

_____

_____

_____

_____

_____

_____

DAY 41

"I am the bread that gives life. No one who comes to me will ever be hungry. No one who believes in me will ever be thirsty."

—John 6:35 (ERV)

JESUS'S WORDS TODAY are from His discourse on the "bread of life following the miraculous feeding of the five thousand. The multitudes tracked Jesus down and wanted to make Him king right then and there. But Jesus knew their hearts were not looking for the promised Messiah, the Savior of the world. Rather, He knew their hearts were desiring only a king who could provide food. They were looking for a king to fulfill fleshly desires rather than the spiritual desires of our hearts. The discourse follows a night where His disciples endured a tremendous storm on the Sea of Galilee and Jesus appeared walking on water, displaying that He is much more than a king. He is 'the Lord of the universe.

In His discourse on the bread of life, Jesus distinguishes between those who seek after the flesh and material things of the world and those who seek after spiritual things. The crowd was seeking the gift not the giver of the gift. Jesus is basically saying, "you seek me not because you saw [or perceived] but because you were filled with food. You missed the real meaning of the miracle." He then exhorts the crowd to not labor for the food that perishes but to labor for the food which endures unto everlasting life. Jesus makes a distinct reference to the manna in the wilderness (Exod. 16), the food God provided in the dessert, but it was not good enough. The children of Israel complained and desired more.

Like the Israelites of old, we too are inclined to labor after the material things we think will provide us with peace and happiness. We think money, success, power, relationships, social acceptance will satisfy us, and we labor after these things. But like manna they satisfy only for a moment and then they spoil and perish. The Samaritan woman at the well wanted the living water offered only so she would not have to ever draw water again—a free ride in life. Jesus is telling us rather to labor after spiritual things, to labor after Him as the way, the truth, the life and in Him you will find more than food and water, more than shelter from the storm. You will find sustenance for all of life's situations. Jesus says, "I am the bread of life" (John 6:35). His words "*I am* are the same words Jehovah used to describe Himself when speaking to Moses at the burning bush. Jesus is telling the world that He is the only true bread, and He invites all to "come and believe and you will never hunger or thirst (spiritually) in this world again. Your peace will be your purpose, and your happiness will be your joy in life.

In the parable of the prodigal son, we find a young man leaving home seeking a better life for himself. But his interpretation of a better life, the good life, was seeking materialism. He sought out fine clothes, jewelry, and good food and drink. It all perished as he spent his entire inheritance trying to be satisfied with the material things of the world. Yet upon returning home with only the tattered clothes he was wearing, his father lovingly ordered the best robe be brought and put on him and that sandals be brought for him. Having lost all his wealth, his father has his servants put a ring on his hand and to prepare a great feast! (Luke 15).

As the bread of life, Jesus is redeemer of lost lives. What was wasted becomes sustainable in Him. The son sought and labored for material peace and happiness and was left with only misery, having no purpose in life, no joy, and no rest in his soul. But our God, our great Father in heaven sent us the true manna, His son Jesus Christ, as the bread of life for us. To those who believe and trust and labor after Him and His truth, you will never hunger nor thirst again. You will know purpose in life and be satisfied and joyful in it.

THOUGHTS

_____

_____

_____

_____

_____

_____

_____

PRAYER

_____

_____

_____

_____

_____

_____

DAY 42

"God looked at everything he had made,
and he saw that everything was very good."

—Genesis 1:31 (ERV)

AT THE HEART of God is His goodness to people. Because God is pure, perfect, holy, and good in all His ways, it is His heart, nature, and longing to pour out blessings and joy upon us. We see the evidence of such goodness from the beginning of creation. He created the light and proclaimed that it was good (Gen. 1:4). He created the dry lands and the seas and saw that it was good (Gen. 1:10). The earth grew grass, plants, and grains, fruit trees, all having seed of its own kind, and God saw that it was good (Gen. 1:12). He placed the sun and moon and stars in the sky to shine over the day and night and saw that it was good (Gen. 1:18). God filled the seas with many living things and the sky with birds and saw that it was good (Gen. 1:21). He made every kind of animal, and it was good (Gen. 1:25). Upon creating humans in His own image, God gave all of His creation to them and from our passage today we see that God looked at everything He had made and saw that everything was very good. Not just good but very good. In Genesis 1:25 the Bible describes God's reaction as it being suitable, pleasant, and He approved of it completely. God's creation was very good and pleasing to Him because He saw it as very good for you and me. It was all created for our benefit. The goodness of God is to bless us and fill our lives with immense joy.

God's goodness has continued from creation to this very day. His goodness is the same goodness that appeared in glory to Moses (Ex. 33:19). The same goodness the Psalmist declares that shall follow us all or our days (Ps. 23:6). A goodness that is seen in the land of the living and to those who are His (Ps. 27:13). God's glorious splendor and majesty is full of wonderous works and awesome acts that declare his goodness (Ps. 145:5–7). God's goodness is the invitation to taste and see that the Lord is good (Ps. 34:8), and His goodness is for all who truly fear and trust God (Ps. 31:19). The essence of God is mistakenly good and therefore our goodness as His creation can only come from Him. Gloriously manifested in us through salvation in Jesus Christ, the son of God who died for our sins because it was not only good for us, but the only and best plan of eternal righteousness for us.

God's goodness is not just for humanity in general but offered personally in relationship with God through Jesus. God is good to you and pours out His goodness upon you and your life. So beloved of God, rejoice in His goodness today. Stand fast in knowing God is good and desires good for you. His thoughts and plans are for your well-being and peace, not to bring you disaster and evil. He will give you a future and hope, an expected end of goodness to your life (Jer. 29:11).

Beloved of God, open your heart today and let the fullness of His goodness come into your life, and reign in your life, in Jesus's name. Amen.

THOUGHTS

_____

_____

_____

_____

_____

_____

PRAYER

_____

_____

_____

_____

_____

_____

DAY 43

"This shall be the covenant that I will make with the house of Israel; After those days, saith the LORD, I will put my law in their inward parts, and I write in their hearts; and will be their God, and they shall be my people."

—Jeremiah 31:33 (KJV)

GOD IS SO good. We find throughout the Bible covenants whereby God has established and continues to establish His loving relationship with His people. It is because of the goodness of God the He establishes, keeps, and fulfills His covenants with us and that we as His people can stand in faith and hope as we enter in and partake in His glorious goodness.

In the Bible, we find five major covenants of God declaring the goodness of His redemptive plan for a fallen people. The first is the Noahic covenant (Gen. 9) when God resets His creative work after the flood and promises to Noah to preserve all living creatures and never to destroy them again with a flood. The sign of that covenant is the rainbow. The second is the Abrahamic covenant (Gen. 12 and 15) when God promises to give Abraham a land and many descendants that will form a great nation. The third covenant is the Mosaic covenant, when God after leading the people out of the slavery and bondage of Egypt, gives the Law (Exod. 20) to the people and promises that if they keep the law, they will be blessed. If they don't keep the law, they will be cursed. The fourth covenant is the Davidic covenant, when God promises King David that his line would have no end, and that the Messiah will come from his descendants.

These four major covenants all lead us to the fifth major covenant from God and the testimony of God's goodness to humanity by way of the New Covenant. As our passage today shows, it is God's promise to rescue His people from the bondage of sin as portrayed by the exiled people of God in Babylon. It is the promise and fulfillment of a Savior, Lord, and King, the Messiah who would bring unconditional forgiveness of sin through the renewing of the hearts of His people. It is the new way where knowledge of God becomes personal and intimate, not written on tablets of stone or parchment but on the hearts of humans. At the Last Supper Jesus took the cup and said, "this is the new covenant in My blood, which is shed for you" (Luke 22:20 NKJV).

The death and resurrection of Jesus Christ is the fulfillment of God's plan of redemption as promised to His people. It is the new creation one becomes as a redeemed person of God. The old way of sin and regret and shame is past, buried, and forgiven. The new way of life lived in joy and hope and assurance is in Jesus Christ who has reconciled us to God (2 Cor. 5:17–18).

Therefore, as God has reconciled mankind to Him through Christ, the Bible calls on us to go forth as His ambassadors of reconciliation to share with the world the good news of salvation.

You are a new creation in Christ, beloved of God. Go forth and declare the goodness of God's redemptive plan! In Jesus's name. Amen.

THOUGHTS

PRAYER

DAY 44

"For we are his workmanship, created in Christ Jesus for good works, which God prepared ahead of time for us to do."

—Ephesians 2:10 (CSB)

DO YOU CONSIDER your salvation a form of worship? Years ago, I was blessed with an unexpected bonus from work, and I felt led to buy a beautiful piece of jewelry for my wife's birthday, which was a rare event in our household. I was apprehensive entering the jewelry store. Seeing the prices made me even more apprehensive, but I kept looking and was drawn to a beautiful ring and bracelet set in gold with rainbow-colored gemstones. Admiring the glow and beauty of the set I asked the salesperson about the gems. They were iolite, amethyst, garnet, citrine, peridot, and blue topaz. I immediately thought of the gems adorning the foundations of New Jerusalem described in Revelation 21 and knew immediately this was to be my purchase.

When buying jewelry, they always present it on a black velvet background so you can fully appreciate its beauty. Such is a picture of our passage today in that before we can appreciate the great and awesome glory of God's work in our lives, we must first see ourselves for what we were, the black velvet background. Before Christ, we were dead in our trespasses and sin, living a life in darkness separated from God. But in Christ, we are God's treasure, new creations of His glorious salvation. Diamonds plucked from the rough shining in all the glory of His salvation.

But salvation is not just a celebration of being transformed from the darkness of the past. It's not just about what we are saved from, but equally about what we are saved for. The word *workmanship* in our verse of the day is the Greek word *poiema* where we get the English word *poem*. It implies that once saved, we are God's works of art. Salvation is not through our work but through the work of God (vv. 8–9), God's elect are beautiful pieces of art created to worship Him and demonstrate the light to a dark world. Salvation is not just about deliverance; it's also about transformation, a glorious transformation to be seen, shared, and heard. We are works of art expressing adoring worship to an adoring creator. We are His instruments of praise to the world. The true expression of love, mercy, and grace as God's glorious workmanship.

Before finalizing the purchase of my wife's jewelry, I asked the salesperson to put it on and show me it in the sunlight. Wow! That was the image that sealed the deal. Glistening so beautifully in the sunlight it is a picture of you, beloved of Christ, as an expression of your walk and worship in the light of God. You are His workmanship, His beautiful piece of art, a gemstone in the rough culled from utter darkness, now shining in the light of His glory to be seen and appreciated as an expressive act of worship.

THOUGHTS

_____

_____

_____

_____

_____

_____

PRAYER

_____

_____

_____

_____

_____

_____

DAY 45

"And they were in the way going up to Jerusalem;
and Jesus went before them: and they were amazed;
and as they followed, they were afraid."

—Mark 10:32 (KJV)

JESUS AND THE disciples are on the move. From the valley of Judea across the Jordan River up to Jerusalem. A journey upward of some thirty-five hundred feet. Our Lord had already spoken before of His imminent death to the disciples. He gives them more details as the religious leaders in Jerusalem would condemn Him to death and deliver Him to the gentiles (v. 33). Then they would mock and spit on Him (v. 34) before crucifying Him. Ultimately, He would rise from the dead to life again. The glorious and joyful moment of victory over death.

As I read this verse, I thought of our own faith journey in our Lord's walk to Jerusalem. Faith is a climb as we continually move upward in our strength of faith, purity of faith, and peace of faith in our journey through life as a Christian. The climb can be graceful and easy at times, but it can also be challenging and difficult. We take heart, though, in our Lord as we find courage and strength in this moment. He is ascending to Jerusalem to begin His week of passion in saving mankind. He will knowingly face physical and emotional atrocities. And yet we see our Lord going ahead of the disciples with vigor and determination, leading them forward, moving toward God's will for the redemption of all.

I think of all the brave soldiers who have run into battle with rifles and bayonets determined to mete out victory over their enemy combatants. I am touched by the fireman and first responders who sped toward ground zero on 9/11 and the many who then climbed the twin towers determined to rescue the victims of the catastrophe playing out live to the entire world. I am in awe of the Christian workers around the world courageously and enthusiastically carrying on the work of the Lord in spite of persecution, suffering, condemnation, and even death.

Whatever your journey of faith, beloved of Christ, the Lord is leading your climb yesterday, today, and forever. He is showing you the strength and determination, dedication and sovereignty of God who is in full control of your journey. Even if the climb seems to be too much, the Lord is with you. The apostle Paul concludes his letter to the Romans: "For I reckon that the sufferings of this present time are not worthy to be compared with the glory of which shall be revealed to us" (Rom. 8:18 KJV). The disciples were amazed how Jesus had so much energy moving ahead of them on the climb to Jerusalem. It says in our verse they were also afraid as they followed behind. Perhaps Jesus and the disciples had the prophet Isaiah's words in mind when he said, "I will let those people beat me and pull the hair from my beard. I will not hide my face when they say bad things to me and spit at me. The Lord God will help and the bad things they say about me will not hurt me. I will be strong. I know I will not be disappointed" (Isa. 50:6–7 ERV).

The disciples knew intuitively this journey to Jerusalem would not be like any other. Their fears were real, but their strength was fortified in Jesus. So be encouraged, beloved of Christ. Be thankful and be grateful. You are chosen of God for the journey set before you in faith. He reigns over all things. His kingdom is close. His plan is righteous, and it was Jesus who sped to the cross for you.

THOUGHTS

_____

_____

_____

_____

_____

_____

PRAYER

_____

_____

_____

_____

_____

_____

_____

DAY 46

"But let patience have her perfect work, that ye may be
perfect and complete, lacking nothing."

—James 1:4 (KJV)

JAMES BEGINS HIS letter speaking to the church about the trials and temptations they will face. He says to count it all joy knowing the testing of your faith produces patience. Other translations use the word *endurance* for patience. I love how the Greek word is in the female gender reinforcing how women and men complement each other in God's perfecting work in us.

Patience and endurance are the result of faith manifested in the believer's everyday life. Trials and temptations are what mature one's faith. I don't like trials and temptations, as I am sure you don't either, and I find it difficult to count them as joy. But God allows them to strengthen us, to make us more like Jesus. They prepare us for heaven by giving us an assurance of God's goodness and expectancy of living in glory in the future.

The perfecting work of patience and endurance is amazingly proclaimed in the testimony of Noah and his family. The Bible says Noah prior to the flood was a man of great faith with a real relationship with God. Noah had done all that the Lord had commanded him to do. So one day God tells Noah to build a boat because all that moisture in the sky is going to come down and the springs from below will burst upward. And the boat should be the size of a football field. (You don't know what that is, Noah, but it's about 134 by 22 meters.) And by the way, it will take some one hundred years to build. Can you imagine the trials and temptations Noah and his family endured all those years? They were the joke of their community, no doubt mocked and laughed at. Perhaps donkey and cart tours were showing up at the site to get a look at the "crazy" family. But through all the pain and suffering, the warfare from the people, the building challenges, the family doubts, the temptations to call it a day and go back to the wages of the world, Noah and his family endured with patience and were saved.

When Jesus comes again, I want to be found in the ark of God's grace too. I want my heart to be found ready and waiting, having patiently endured the fiery trials and tribulations, the temptations and sufferings of life. At the end of his letter, James condemns the ways of the world and exhorts believers to be patient until the Lord's coming like the farmer waiting for the early and late rains (James 5:7–8). The righteous will always have to be patient and endure, but in time, and I believe it'll be sooner rather than later, Jesus will come and right all wrongs. Like the cat on the poster, "hang in there, baby." Hang in there, beloved of God. And for the guys, learn from your mothers, spouses, sisters, and others on the virtues and blessings of patience and endurance.

THOUGHTS

PRAYER

DAY 47

"But I trust in your faithful love, Lord. I will be happy
when you save me. Then I will sing to the LORD because
he was so good to me."

—Psalm 13:5–6 (ERV)

PSALM 13 IS a song that concludes with a beautiful proclamation of trust and rejoicing. But the psalm does not start out
that way. The author and songwriter David begins with a series
of lamentations. How long will you forget me, Lord? Will it be
forever? How long will your refuse to accept me? How long must
I wonder if you have forgotten me? How long do I have to feel
sadness in my heart? How long will my enemies keep having
victory over me?

Who among us as believers have not struggled with such
painful questions from the heart? Yet we know it takes patience
and endurance to live our lives for God. The Bible tells us that
patience works perfection in our lives (James 1:4–8). Abraham
and Sarah are an amazing example of God's goodness and
redemptive purpose through much patience. Abraham received
the promise from God that a great nation would come from
his descendants. The problem was that Sarah was barren with
no children and Abraham was seventy-five years old. They
waited patiently. Twenty-five years they waited after hearing the
promise and then they tried to move ahead of God's timetable
after Sarah gave up in her heart. Such sorrow no doubt followed
many prayers and cries of how long O Lord? But the promise
came from the one and only true God, the One who cannot lie.
Deep down Abraham did not waiver in belief (Rom. 4:20–21).
In the end their patience was perfected as God provided the
promised heir.

It was, and is, and continues to be the purpose of God that true believers will be saved through faith. Life as a believer will be a journey of trials and tribulations as we are being perfected in faith the same way God worked His perfection in the lives of Abraham and Sarah. Although you may be crying how long O Lord? How long before I get an answer to this or that issue? How long must I endure through this trial? This temptation? This suffering? But God sees it all. He sees even when our patience is waning. But He never forgets or forsakes you. He always accepts you just as you are. He is always ready to forgive you. Sorrows will turn to joy. In the meantime, sing! Rejoice for you are saved unto an eternity with the everlasting Lord. Look at all the good He has done in your life and sing.

David's psalm is intended to be sung together by the children of Israel. It speaks to the common experiences we have as believers today whereby we find comfort in the presence of others as we sing and share with one another. Rejoice and cry together. Exhort, encourage, and pray with each other. In the way of fellowship our patience and endurance are strengthened. Let us not forget. God is patiently waiting for the last soul to be saved (2 Pet. 3:9). He continues to work on behalf of those who wait for Him (Isa. 44:4). So sing, beloved of Christ. Sing out in the midst of the congregation as well as the quiet times of your meditations and prayers. The Lord has heard the cries of my weeping. The Lord has heard the pleas for my help. The Lord has received my prayers (Ps. 6:8–9).

THOUGHTS

_____

_____

_____

_____

_____

_____

PRAYER

_____

_____

_____

_____

_____

_____

DAY 48

"Dear friends, we should love each other,
because love comes from God."

—1 John 4:7 (ERV)

CHURCH TRADITION TELLS us that the apostle John, when he was feeble and almost completely blind, was carried from church to church to share the profound wisdom and experiences from his time with Jesus. Often, the younger people would clamor to see and speak with John on his visits. It is told when asked what is the most important thing to know as a Christian, John would stress to love one another just as Jesus taught (John 13:34).

With all the confusion and chaos going on in the world today it is easy for one to be cynical and judgmental toward the world and people. But as messed up as people and the world can be, there is one constant: God is love. Love is not God as some would want you to believe. God created us in His image to not only be loved but to love others. Much of the problem with the world and people is their concept of love is without God, and they end up looking to fill their need to be loved and love in all the wrong places.

Our passage speaks to the one true love, which is God's love. The apostle John tells us God is the one true source of love. Just as light and heat flow from the sun, so does true love flow from God. It is a love that provides the believer with strength for the day, rest from the labor, light for the way, and grace in the struggles. The good news is that this love from God has been bestowed on us through Jesus Christ, the full embodiment of God's love.

John goes from testifying that God is not only the source of true love, but also that God is the true giver of love (1 John 4:9–10). From the beginning of time God has been the source of love. It has been said that where creation is the "heart" of God's love to us, His word is the "heart" of His love to us. It is only that heart of love who sent His son, the Word, who died for us. This is true love.

So with God as the source and giver of true love, John goes on to share that such love of God will be evidenced by our practice of God's love. To know God's love is to share God's love. To share God's love is to practice God's love. To practice God's love is to love one another (1 John 4:11–12). Previously the apostle shares that hate is impossible with God's people (1 John 3:15). As with Jesus, there is to be no place in our heart for hate, but only love manifested through repentance, grace, mercy, compassion, caring, and sharing. God's love is real and sincere. When we love with God's love, it is not to be done for the glory of men but for the glory of God.

Beloved of God, as we navigate a world that so desperately wants to be loved but is blind to the need for God's true love, let our hearts be found full of compassion and humility that the world sees the true love of God in us and pouring out of us. As Jesus showed us the way of God's love, let us be the lights of that way bringing people to the place of what they really need, which is God's love.

THOUGHTS

_____

_____

_____

_____

_____

_____

PRAYER

_____

_____

_____

_____

_____

_____

DAY 49

"Jesus wept"

—John 11:35

"JESUS WEPT." THE shortest verse in the Bible. His weeping is not like that of the mourners over the death of Lazarus, but rather it is a bursting into tears, a sudden outburst of emotion from deep pain within the heart. On two occasions in the Bible Jesus is found weeping. When Jesus entered Jerusalem on the colt, he burst into tears, an audible sobbing in another sudden outburst of deep emotion from the heart as He wept over His beloved city of Jerusalem (Luke 19:41), a city whose leaders and people have and will continue to reject Him and His saving words of salvation.

On both occasions in John and Luke Jesus weeps over death. The death of His beloved city that will come in AD 70 at the hands of Roman Emperor Titus and his soldiers, as prophesied by Micah: "Zion shall be plowed like a field, Jerusalem shall become heaps of ruins" (Mic. 3:12 NKJV). Here in John 11 Jesus is weeping over the grave of Lazarus, knowing that God's creation was never to suffer the sting of death. Death was not to be part of life, but the fall of man brought it to this world and all in it. I recall years ago when arriving to the East Coast from California answering the call to plant a new church. As I was driving to work one day watching the faces of the drivers in the cars going by the other way, I was overwhelmed with the despair and sorrow of how they all needed Jesus in their life, and I burst out crying in my car knowing that many will die in their sin rather than in the grace of God.

The good news is that although we see so much death in life, so much pain, and our sorrow as believers will be emotional and probably take the form of tearful outbursts, our sorrow still has hope attached to our tears. It is the hope that comes with abiding in God's love. Paul says, "Ye sorrow not as others which have no hope." (1 Thess. 4:13 KJV). This is the simple faith we as believers are to share to the world. There is hope in Jesus Christ. Death is not the end game for professing Christians. There is no tragedy in death for those in Christ. To go to heaven is to live forever in joy and peace. "O death where is thy sting? O grave where is thy victory? The sting of death is sin; and the strength of sin is the law. But thanks be to God, which giveth us the victory through our Lord Jesus Christ" (1 Cor. 15:55–56 KJV).

Rather than the sorrow of death, Jesus invites us out of the grave, turn from sin and rejection, and come to Him. Come into the saving grace and knowledge of Him. And then He says go. Upon the resurrection of Lazarus, he was to go into the world and declare the new life unconstrained by the graveclothes of death. Go into the world and declare the good news of life in Christ, a life of hope and love being dead to sin, now living in the new life of grace and peace.

Jesus wept. But He rejoices in the life-giving power of the resurrection. As with Lazarus who became a living witness to this life-giving power of Christ, so too are you, beloved, to be a witness of Christ's resurrection power over death unto eternal life.

THOUGHTS

_____

_____

_____

_____

_____

_____

PRAYER

_____

_____

_____

_____

_____

_____

_____

DAY 50

"But I have a few things against thee."

—Revelation 2:14 (KJV)

THE APOSTLE JOHN'S third letter to the seven churches follows the letters to the loveless church in Ephesus and the persecuted church in Smyrna. In whole the seven letters represent a historical snapshot of the church in that day and as many scholars believe a view of the church in our present and future days. John's third letter is to the church in Pergamum (Pergamos). A leading city in the political and cultural arena also known for its passion in seeking of knowledge. It was also a pagan city that worshiped many different gods. From John's letter Jesus is rebuking the church for being a compromising church. Historically, the church in Pergamos represents the church in the post persecution era from approximately AD 325 to AD 570. It is the era of the first state sponsored church when state religion is suddenly placed on people who were not believers, which led to compromising values, compromising religious practices, and compromising beliefs.

The Lord begins by commending the church in Pergamos for their good works in the midst of a city filled with paganism. He says, I know your works, even where Satan has set up shop, but you are holding up the name of Jesus and keeping to your faith (v. 13). But like most of the other letters Jesus speaks rebuke to the church in Pergamos saying, "I have a few things against you." The rebuke, followed by His correction, is aimed at those who joined the church and brought with them strange doctrines and practices. False worship and offerings to idols, and church leaders lording it over the flock. The church's acceptance was its compromise. Much like today where we see so much practice and acceptance of worldly moral values and sin in the church.

The church is to be the example to the world of God's holiness and purity. As Christians we are to be such examples as well to the world. But when we compromise godly standards of holiness and purity, we are actually putting up stumbling blocks for others to fail in their faith or not really have true faith to begin with. They need to "repent," the Lord says (v. 16), and the remedy is to go forward walking in truth and love without compromise. The brilliant author and theologian G. K. Chesterton once quipped, "Compromise used to mean that half a loaf of bread was better than no bread. Among modern statesmen it seems to now mean that half a loaf of bread is better than a whole loaf."

Dearest beloved of Christ, compromise is never the way forward for the truth and love of God. As one follows the progression of John's seven letters to the churches, we see a pattern where in the first letter lovelessness seems to invite persecution upon the church. The very nature of persecution invites compromise to relieve the suffering. Compromise, however, will lead to corruption and corruption leads to a dead church, as we see in the church in Sardis. Let you and I not be found by our Lord with a compromising faith and compromising hearts. Rather, let us be found shining brightly in the uncompromised truth and uncompromising love of Jesus Christ. Let us be His children, no longer tossed by the waves and "blown around by every wind of doctrine, by human cunning with cleverness in the techniques of deceit. But speaking the truth in love; let us grow in every way into Him who is the head—Christ (Eph. 4:14–15 CSB).

THOUGHTS

_____

_____

_____

_____

_____

_____

PRAYER

_____

_____

_____

_____

_____

_____

DAY 51

"The steadfast love of the LORD never ceases,
his mercies never come to an end; they are new every morning:
great is your faithfulness. The LORD is my portion,
says my soul, therefore I will hope in him."

—Lamentations 3:22–25 (ESV)

AS ONE SURVEYS the landscape of life and all its troubles, sufferings, and challenges, we know there is always hope for the believer. The Lord is always the source of hope. The Lord is our portion, which may be a reference to a time past in Canaan when the land was portioned out among the different tribes. It was there that Aaron and the priestly tribe of the Levites were given no land, but instead the Lord said: "I am your portion and your inheritance among the people of Israel" (Num. 18:20 ESV). It is a picture of a special and personal relationship with God as the priests were set apart in service to Him. It is the same relationship with God that inspired the psalmist to proclaim through a crisis that God is "my portion forever!" (Ps. 73:26 ESV).

A personal relationship with God is the foundation of one's faith and the essence of one's hope. Such divine hope exists by knowing the true character of God.

Our passage comes from a time past, but faith brings it into an experience with God that can be had in the present. God's character—yesterday, today, and forever—is that of a steadfast love, promising the faithful He has been and always will be with His people and His love for them never changes. God's mercies speak to His compassion toward His people, which never ends and is our salvation. "Because of our God's merciful compassion, the dawn from on high will visit us to shine on those who live in darkness and the shadow of death, to guide our feet into the way of peace" (Luke 1:78–79 CSB). And He is faithful. It is God's faithfulness where we can rest in hope. A faithfulness that never fails. When he received the ten commandments the Lord spoke to Moses saying, "The Lord—the Lord is a compassionate and gracious God, slow to anger and abounding in faithful love and truth" (Exod. 34:6 CSB).

Love, mercy, and faithfulness are traits of God that are available and new every morning no matter your sins of yesterday or the trouble, the suffering, the challenges today. God is there for us each and every day. Each new day is a blessed do over. One is given a fresh anointing and power and strength and courage to get through. And for those who believe, each day is an opportunity to walk in a fresh, personal, loving relationship with God. He and He alone is our portion. He is all we need. Christ is the aroma and assurance of God's steadfast love, mercies, and faithfulness. His death and resurrection took relationship with God from the past into the present, where He is with you every day, if you let Him.

THOUGHTS

_____

_____

_____

_____

_____

_____

PRAYER

_____

_____

_____

_____

_____

_____

_____

DAY 52

"Only those whose names are written in the Lamb's book of life will enter the city."

—Revelation 21:27 (ERV)

THIS PAST YEAR my wife and I have been astonished as we thought some event or activity happened a year or so ago only to realize in actuality it took place three or four years ago. The lost years of COVID and all the chaos that came with those years. Unfortunately, for far too many people these past few years have been a time of lost hope. A lost hope for the present as well as the future. To many, they feel that hope has been canceled in their hearts.

Hope has and never will be lost or canceled for the Christian. In Exodus 32:32 we find the first mention of God's book of life. It is a divine ledger of the citizens of the kingdom community, God's people of Israel. The passage speaks also of some who have sinned against God and there is a blotting out of those names from the book. Such action by God in the erasing of names from the ledger indicates a loss of citizenship and fellowship with God. But the good news is that for those in Christ our citizenship is in heaven as we eagerly await the Lord's return from heaven (Phil. 3:20). Our names are written in the divine ledger of heaven known as the Lamb's book of life. I recently heard a pastor liken this truth of becoming and being a Christian when God cuts our names from the book of life and then pastes it into the Lamb's book of life.

Where the Old Testament book of life implies privilege and the partaking in temporary blessings from God's kingdom, the Lamb's book of life does not imply, but rather ensures those in Christ of the privilege and partaking in the present eternal blessings of God's heavenly kingdom. Such is the blessed faith and hope of the true Christian (Heb. 11:1). Heaven, not earth, is our hope as believers. Heaven is our victory. As Jesus told us: "Let not your heart be troubled, you believe in God, believe also in Me. In My Father's house are many mansions, if it were not so, I would have told you. I go to prepare a place for you (John 14:1–2 NKJV).

Beloved of Christ, putting one's hope in the fleeting things and people of the world will only lead to lost years and regret in what you could have done for Christ. Instead, let your hope of eternity be your joy. Set your heart on the above as a heavenly minded person whose citizenship is in the kingdom of heaven and whose name shall never be blotted out of the Lamb's book of life.

THOUGHTS

PRAYER

DAY 53

"But by the grace of God, I am what I am".

—1 Corinthians 15:10 (KJV)

I AM WHAT I am. What are you? Who are you? For me, I can say I am a sinner saved by grace and I thank God it was of His doing and not up to my doings.

Are you thankful today for what God has done for you? A great theologian once said: "If my children wake up on Christmas morning and have somebody to thank for putting candy in their stockings, have I no one to thank for putting two feet in mine?" I love that. So simple and yet so eternally profound. I would add to this statement being thankful for also keeping two feet in my stockings.

Thankfulness begins with knowing what God as already done for you and it starts with grace. Grace is getting what you don't deserve. It is the unmerited favor of God to those who deserve the opposite, which is all of us for "all have sinned and fall short of the glory of God." (Rom. 3:23 NKJV). This grace must be received in one's heart to truly understand God. Grace should also be on our minds constantly in attitudes of thanks to lead us in our lives. A life of thankfulness is not about giving more, praying more, studying more, or serving more. Such are the natural expressions of thankfulness to what God has done for you already. He loved you so much in that while you were still a sinner, He died for you (Rom. 5:8). Jesus died for us to pay the price for our sins willingly in grace. He then rose from the dead and ascended to the right hand of Father God where He makes intercession for you out of love for you. The Bible says Jesus prays for you continually (unmerited favor). His thoughts toward you are good and not evil (unmerited favor). He forgives you of your sins (unmerited favor). He leads you and guides you through life as you choose to follow (unmerited favor). He empowers you with the Holy Spirit (unmerited favor). All the while as He prepares an eternal home for you in heaven (unmerited favor). Amazing grace, how sweet the sound!

With grace in your heart and forever on your mind let thankfulness rule your days. I am what I am, a child of God, and I will thank the Lord with all my heart. I will declare all His wondrous works. I will rejoice and boast about Him. I will sing about Your name, Lord most high (Ps. 9:1–2).

THOUGHTS

_____

_____

_____

_____

_____

_____

PRAYER

_____

_____

_____

_____

_____

_____

DAY 54

"The living, only the living can thank you, as I do today.
A Father will make your faithfulness known to children."

—Isaiah 38:19 (CSB)

IN OUR VERSE today, we find King Hezekiah sick and facing imminent death. Helpless and no doubt depressed, he prayed to God and in answer to that prayer God promised to extend his life another fifteen years. God would use King Hezekiah to lead Judah through a season of conflict with Assyria. The king understood that God had ordained his sickness for his faith to be strengthened as it would need to be in the years ahead. His response to this miracle of God was to sing out praise. He was alive and promised to commit to praising God not only privately before his family and children but also corporately in the temple.

"The living, only the living" is a statement about relationship with God. The living can praise a god but only one who is alive spiritually can praise the true God in spirit and truth (John 4:23–24). For the believer today, to praise God in spirit and truth is to be in Christ. One's righteous standing and relationship with God is through Jesus Christ. It is by His grace and mercy that one is saved despite being unworthy. As I am a sinner today unworthy of God's grace and mercy, I am yet saved and alive in Christ. So I will thank Him and praise Him all my days and proclaim His name to whosoever will hear, in the public square and in the privacy of my home.

It is generally agreed that Hezekiah had no children at this time but knew the value of parents' influence. He declares that fathers are to share their faith and thankfulness to God with their children and to let them know of the faithfulness of God's promises, which are for every generation.

Beloved in Christ, be sure to take the time this day to sincerely thank and praise our Lord God who is your very breath and life as you hold on to the confession of your faith without wavering for your God who promised is faithful (Heb. 10:23). And be sure to tell someone about it.

THOUGHTS

PRAYER

DAY 55

"Come now and let us reason together, saith the Lord:
though your sins be as scarlet, they shall be as white as snow;
though they be red like crimson, they shall be as wool."

—Isaiah 1:18 (KJV)

IN THE AGE of technology, devices are used to save us from effort and labor, suffering and pain. Unfortunately, we have become dependent on such technologies and created a selfish culture oozing with sentiment and good works, and our religion embraces grace but lacks any sacrifice. There is a religious culture that honors, praises, and even imposes the so-called faith from politicians, world leaders, liberal scholars, pop and rock stars, and all sorts of entertainers that have sprung up from the new world of internet influencers. Christianity has become a cafeteria style smorgasbord of beliefs one can chose or reject to fit their lifestyles wrought with fleshly desires and sin.

The God of the Bible, however, views sin in a very clear and direct way. There is one way of cleansing and redemption, and our passage today states the way to receive true grace as opposed to culturally cheap grace. To the old testament saints, sin was never an abstract thought. Sin was considered a great burden that needed lifting. It was recognized as walking the crooked path that needed to be straightened (Isa. 59:8, Pro. 15:21). And sin was likened unto a red stain that needed cleansing. In the prophet Isaiah's day, a scarlet stain was impossible to remove from fabric. Just as impossible to remove was sin within one's soul. But by God's grace and mercy He sent a Redeemer who, as declared by the prophet, is the way of true cleansing, the only way to cleanse our souls one dark blot.

Let us reason together. The invitation to all sinners is to accept the reasonable solution of the gospel of redemption through Jesus Christ. It is not an invitation to cheap café grace. It is not for discussion, debate, or round table forums. It is not for theological and seminary positioning. It is the reasonable and only solution as we stand guilty before a righteous judge with Jesus Christ as our advocate and substitute redeemer. It is divine reasoning we accept in faith.

THOUGHTS

_____

_____

_____

_____

_____

_____

_____

PRAYER

_____

_____

_____

_____

_____

_____

_____

DAY 56

"And, having made peace through the blood of his cross,
by him to reconcile all things unto himself; by him, I say,
whether they be things in earth or things in heaven."

—Colossians 1:20 (KJV)

AS I PONDER and pray this morning about all that's going on in the world and the stresses of terrorism, war, division, spiritual attacks corporately and personally, I can honestly say with confidence it is well with my soul because I have hope. I have hope because I know I have victory, and I know I have victory because of the Cross of Jesus Christ. "But God forbid that I should glory except in the cross of our Lord Jesus Christ, by whom the world is crucified to me, and I to the world" (Gal. 6:14 NKJV).

Charles Spurgeon once said: "There are a thousand enemies ahead of you, but if you look back, there are ten-thousand enemies behind you." The answer to our problems in the world and in our lives lie not in man or woman but in Jesus Christ. He came "not to be ministered unto, but to minister, and to give his life a ransom for many" (Matt. 20:28 KJV). Today, it feels like never before the cross to the world and natural person is an offense. But to the believer, the cross is to be the thing above all things in which we glory. The cross is our only hope for today.

Christ died for me. I must live for Him. He is the way, the truth, and my life (John 14:6). In Christ and only in Christ am I in harmony with the divine attributes of God: love and holiness, mercy and grace, truth and righteousness, and ultimately peace, a peace that surpasses all understanding (Phil. 4:7). As Christ was crucified for me, He was also crucified to the world with Himself and us. The fate of the world and all that is opposed to God will be judged, but it is the cross and the cross alone that saves us from judgment. For He is my hope and my peace (Eph. 2:11).

Whatever state you find yourself in today, whatever mood, whatever feeling, whatever trial, whatever condition, the cross is the answer, my friend. The cross is our only hope.

THOUGHTS

_____

_____

_____

_____

_____

_____

PRAYER

_____

_____

_____

_____

_____

_____

DAY 57

"Listen, I am telling you a mystery: We will not all fall asleep,
but we will be changed."

—1 Corinthians 15:51 (CSB)

IN HIS LETTER to the Corinthians, Paul addresses questions
the church had on matters of faith and death as believers in
Christ. Making historical and logical arguments, Paul speaks to
the truths of Christ and the resurrection as evidenced by transformed lives of believers, the truth in the scriptures, and eyewitness testimony to the resurrection. Paul's conclusion is that
without Christ's resurrection, there is no faith for the believer as
our hope is based on this truth.

Paul makes the case that our physical bodies are from earth
and are designed and designated for earth. As such, flesh and
blood cannot inherit the kingdom of God, but our bodies will
be fashioned in likeness to Christ's resurrected glorified body
(Phil. 3:21) for heaven. The Greek word for fashioned means
"clothed from within." Animals have fur, birds have feathers, fish
have scales. All are clothed in their bodies from within, so too
will the beloved of Christ be clothed from within our glorified
bodies. This will be our heavenly bodies transformed from being
sustained by the power of the blood into glorious bodies being
sustained by the power of the spirit.

Paul goes on to tell us the bodily change (transformation)
will occur in a moment, a twinkling of an eye (v. 52). The word
changed (egeiro) means to "rise up" or "rise again." *Strong's
Exhaustive Concordance of the Bible* tells us it means literally to
rise up from sleep, sitting, or lying down. The meaning can be
associated with rising from disease or death or taken figuratively
to mean to rise from obscurity, inactivity, and even from ruins.
Regardless of the meaning, it all points to our great hope we have

in the resurrected Christ. The corruptible earthly body clothed with incorruption. It is further stated by Paul that for those alive in Christ, the transformation will be preceded by a great sound of the trumpet (v. 52)—the rapture of the church as Christ comes for His people. I believe we are on the precipice of this moment. The question to all is *Are you ready*? Are you ready for a glorious party in heaven when those in Christ will be eternal testimonies proclaiming "O death, where is your sting? O grave, where is your victory? The sting of death is sin; and the strength of sin is the law, but thanks be to God who giveth us the victory through our [resurrected] Lord Jesus Christ." (1 Cor. 15:55–57 KJV)

We all sin and fall short of the glory of God (Rom. 3:23). But Christ took our sin and nailed it to the cross so we could be forgiven (Rom. 5:8). He then was resurrected, assuring us we have been forgiven. He paid the punishment. We are alive in Christ and have victory over the eternal grave, which was the sentence on all for sin (John 3:16–17). Receive Him today, beloved. Repent and turn from sin. Salvation is in Christ and Christ alone. Live in His victory and know the things of this world will pass, and the glory of a heavenly world is your future.

Thank you, Jesus, for the hope we have in and through you.

THOUGHTS

PRAYER

DAY 58

"'Absolute futility,' says the Teacher. 'Absolute futility.
Everything is futile.'"

—Ecclesiastes 1:2 (CSB)

ECCLESIASTES IS A book written by King Solomon in his old age. It tells the account of wrestling and struggling with the problems of life. The book is like a guide to deal with the storms of life while barely clinging to one's faith. Solomon rightly concludes in his struggles that faith is the only thing and all would be hopeless without God.

The book begins with a despairing cry over life, "all is futile." All effort, all existence, all accomplishments are one long monotony of work, eating, and sleeping, day after day after day after day and so on. For Solomon, his monotony of life consisted of tasting and experiencing all the sinful pleasures the world can offer and partaking of them all in abundance.

There was no satisfaction; all was futile. There is hopelessness even with all the luxuries and pleasures of life when one is without God. Think of your things in life: a new house or a new car. For our family a new car is a new "used," car and it is so amazing when first purchased. But after time, it is just a car and becomes part of our daily life. Sure, we can be thankful for cars and houses and things but as Solomon points out, there is no hope in the materialism of life. There is no hope in sensual treasures of the world. There is no hope in money, power, or possessions of this world and no true joy if God is not in your life. King Solomon experienced all the world had to offer and none of it provided lasting happiness. In the end, his assessment was that it only made one miserable.

The wise king did discover with life experience, however, that there is hope when there is a true and living relationship with

God. Such is eternal happiness that one can live in. Such hope takes the monotony and mundane of everyday life and turns it into joy unspeakable in our love and service to God.

So remember and reflect, beloved in Christ. When feeling down and in despair, take a look at your life and assess where God is involved in your daily activities. If you have fallen, it is time to pick yourself up. It's time to remember where you came from and who you are in Christ. It's time to lay your life down upon the foundation of your faith. It is time to live your faith again. Living faith needs to be reconstructed in our hearts from time to time so we can see clearly and engage our daily lives in a living hope, not in a false hope found in the things of the world.

"There is hope for those who are still alive—it does not matter who they are. But this saying is true: A living dog is better than a dead lion" (Eccles. 9:4 ERV). As long as there is life, there is hope. Hope in God.

THOUGHTS

_____

_____

_____

_____

_____

_____

_____

PRAYER

_____

_____

_____

_____

_____

_____

_____

DAY 59

"Sorrow is better than laughter; for by the sadness
of the countenance the heart is made better."

—Ecclesiastes 7:3 (KJV)

HOW COULD SORROW possible be better than laughter? Does not the Bible speak to promises of joy, peace, contentment? I would think that a good laugh is always better than sorrow. However, in our passage today, we see the biblical benefit that sorrow can achieve in a person.

As the apostle Paul tells us: "All things work together for good to those who love God and are called according to His purpose." (Rom. 8:28 RTG). *All things* means "all things," including sorrow in our lives. Where laughter is good medicine for the present, sorrow is good medicine for the long haul. Sorrow's benefit is lasting fruit in the lives of believers. Sorrow produces character development and strength of faith, as well as trust in our Lord. As there needs to be a fall and a winter to bring forth the beauty and comfort of spring, so there must be sorrow to bring forth fruits of character and faith that abound and are everlasting.

Sorrow is a process, not an end. Life pressures, loss, affliction, sickness, disease, distress, and all difficulties are used by God to build and strengthen our relationship with Him. We come out of sorrows with a greater dependence on God, and greater trust and belief in the one who saved and saves us. And a greater love for Him. Leaving the upper room heading toward the garden of Gethsemane after sharing with the disciples about His own departure from them, Jesus said: "Truly, truly, I say to you, you will weep and lament, but the world will rejoice. You will be sorrowful, but your sorrow will turn to joy" (John 16:20 ESV) Sorrow came in our Lord's death, but joy came when they saw Him resurrected. Their sad countenance was changed to elation and made better in love, faith, trust, and truth.

Beloved in Christ, whatever tears you have today, know, in time, they lead to triumph of the heart all to the praise and glory of God!

THOUGHTS

PRAYER

DAY 60

"Then the LORD said to Satan, "have you considered
my servant Job?"

—Job 1:8 (NKJV)

RECENTLY I CAME to the end of the book of Job in my personal
Bible reading, and I was troubled with the same thoughts from
previous readings of the book over my thirty-year walk with the
Lord. Why, Lord? Why allow such pain and suffering to one of
your own?

I have read and studied the book of Job many times. I have
heard sermons, read commentaries, used illustrations from the
book in my own sermons and teachings. I get the good from it,
the benefits to the believer. I understand the lessons and applications found it its pages: that God is a sovereign God and in
control, bad things can happen to good people, in suffering one
must never lose hope, friends can fail us, but God does not;
God is with us in the storms and trials of life, just to name a few.
The apostle James tells us Job was a model of perseverance and
patience (James 5:11). Job also provides a warning that in this
world there will be suffering and points to the longing in all of us
for a true mediator with God.

Good stuff, but the agonizing question remained. Why did
it have to be this way with Job, Lord? Coming to the end of the
book, praying and asking for divine inspiration to this question,
I read in where Job is answering the Lord after so much suffering
and before his restoration saying: "In the past I heard about you
[Lord], but now I have seen you with my own eyes, and I am
ashamed of myself. I am so sorry. As I sit in dust and ashes I
promise to change my heart, and my life (Job 42:5–6 ERV). Wow!
It is a true heartfelt confession from Job.

Meditating on this confession I was awakened at 1:19 in the morning as clarity filled my heart about Job and the question Why Lord? I had to get up an write it down. I was directed back to where the Lord told Satan, "have you considered my servant Job?" (Job 1:8 CSB). Satan was looking for a soul to destroy and the verse seems to imply God was offering up Job as a sacrifice to Satan, so he could have his way. Job is described as a good man, a fearful respecter of God who refuses to do evil. Sound familiar? How many Christians today would describe themselves this way?

The Holy Spirit showed me that God was already dealing with Job in their relationship together. Job's confession and repentance confirms there were shortcomings going on. Job apparently had great knowledge of God and was blessed in the peace of God. We see Job admitting that he "heard about" God (Job 42:5), but it is clear Job was lacking in a relationship of true depth and love with God. He knew the benefits of the peace *of* God as those who trust in the Lord benefit from blessings spiritually, mentally, physically, and materially. However, he did not have the fullness of peace, the peace *with* God, which is the ability to experience the peace of God in all things, all circumstances, having a clear conscience (Heb 10:20). God had to strip Job of his blessings before Job would surrender to a right relationship in peace with the Lord. "I heard about you Lord, *but now* I have seen you!" (emphasis mine). It was not a physical sighting but rather a heart sighting in the awareness and knowledge of the true and living God. His confession speaks to Job truly knowing God now and being at total peace with God. Where the relationship was tainted by darkness and the things of the flesh, it is now shinning in a light of brightness he did not know before. Praise be to God!

What about you, beloved of Christ? What about your relationship with God? Is it about your goodness, your dutiful and obedient actions blessed in much peace but lacking in real peace with God because of a shallow relationship with Him? We are all

Jobs. Imperfect creatures but works in progress. In our relationship with God, He desires all of us be in a place where we can experience all of life at peace with God. To get to such a place may just depend on how one is willing to change. For Job, it took the loss of every blessing he had, but it resulted in a beautiful change and restoration in his newfound peace with God. This is what God wants for you, friend. I am not saying you have to lose everything in life like Job, but if that's what it takes. How many flights of stairs must we fall down before looking up to be in complete peace with God? Job got there: "I promise to change my heart, and my life." What about you, friend?

Why Lord? I say why not, beloved of Christ.

THOUGHTS

_____

_____

_____

_____

_____

_____

_____

PRAYER

_____

_____

_____

_____

_____

_____

DAY 61

"In the beginning was the Word."

—John 1:1 (CSB)

THE WORD IN Greek is *logos*, which means more than thought but implies intelligence in that there is no thought without a thinker. In our brief passage today the word (*logos*) is written in the Greek perfect tense which tells us it is continuous, not just a word for the past but also for the present and the future. God's Word (*logos*) is the same yesterday, today, and forever. We are told that the word (*logos*) became flesh and dwelt among us (v. 14). The word is Jesus Christ and became the literal manifestation of God's Word (*logos*). "God who at various times and in various ways spoke in times past to the fathers by the prophets, has in these last days spoken to us by His Son whom He has appointed heir of all things [past, present, and future], through whom also He made the worlds (Heb. 1:1–2 NKJV).

Today with so much progressive theology, winds of doctrine blowing through the church, false teaching for the itchy ears, and vain babblings amongst God's people, John is telling us it is the Word that matters most. The Word, Jesus Christ, is our rock and anchor of faith. It is the thing we must never leave behind. "Anyone who does not remain in Christ's teaching but goes beyond it does not have God. The one who remains in that teaching, this one has both the Father and the Son." (2 John 9 CSB). "And if anyone takes away from the words of the book of this prophecy, God will take away his share of the tree of life and the holy city, which are written about in this book" (Rev. 22:19 CSB).

The only hope, the only path from darkness to light is the *logos*, the Word of God, Jesus Christ. This is the solution for everything that is not of God. The Word is the discerner of good and evil, truth, and lies, and the provider of peace, safety, and wisdom to navigate the increasingly dark and dangerous ways of the world.

Beloved of Christ, we have the truth. The anchor keeping us in place in the midst of any storm. We have the wisdom to apply to all things and the ability in truth to judge and test all things by God's Word (1 John 4:1). Remember Him, remember the Word, the *logos*, and apply it to your life always, and you will fare well in this world.

THOUGHTS

PRAYER

DAY 62

"A bruised reed shall he not break, and the smoking flax shall he not quench; he shall bring forth judgment unto truth."

—Isaiah 42:3 (KJV)

AS A SERVANT of the Lord do you ever feel burnt out, discouraged, depressed, despaired, hopeless, and even broken? I do, and I know you do as well from time to time. This is just the reality of serving Jesus in a world that goes against His truth. The battle has been going on for a long time. Moses was so discouraged and despairing he asked God to just kill him (Num. 11:14–15). David and his men wept and wept over a defeat (1 Sam. 30:4). The apostle Paul listed his ministry woes in his letter to the Corinthians (2 Cor. 11). The prophet Elijah came to a place of exhaustion, unworthiness, and a lost sense of purpose in his dealings with Jezebel (1 Kings 19:14). As Christ suffered, we shall too as His servants. (Rom. 8:17–18)

We've all been there. Perhaps you are there right now. Fear not my friend and let the peace of God that surpasses all understanding comfort you in this season. Paul, reflecting on his ministry journey, tells us he suffered the loss of all things, and concluded that their value was only that of "dung" that he gain so much more in Christ. (Phil. 3:8). Jesus quotes from our passage in Isaiah as He was addressing the rejecters of His truth. The Pharisees seethed over our Lord's works performed on the Sabbath. They plotted to kill Him, and, discerning the danger, Jesus withdrew from the crowds and quoted this passage to the disciples (Matt. 12:20).

I find it interesting that Matthew is the one who captures this moment in history. I believe Matthew was a bruised reed feeling burnt out, perhaps despairing over the ministry challenges on top of his own personal challenges. A dreaded tax collector from the tribe of Levi, he had walked away from his religious heritage to follow Jesus. He became a dreaded outsider now in ministry to the outsiders. But Jesus sees it all. He sees and knows when His servants are weak and despairing, discouraged and depressed, burned out and broken. As Isaiah prophesied about the coming Messiah, our Lord's quoting it brings it into the realm of suffering to all. As Jesus was "bruised for our iniquities" (Isa. 53:5 NKJV), He understands the bruised reed in us. In all His miracle healings Jesus was ministering to a bruised reed. He ministered to the bruised reeds gathered in the upper room after His death. He restored Peter after denying the Lord. God will never despise a broken spirit or contrite heart (Ps. 51:17). He will not despise the prayers of the destitute (Ps. 102:17).

A bruised reed He shall not break is a picture of one bent and broken in the service of the Lord. Overwhelmed but how gloriously peaceful knowing it is Jesus who promises to mend and restore the bruised reed. *A smoking flax He shall not quench* is a picture of barely hanging in there in one's service to the Lord. You may feel like your fire is gone, like your zeal and passion are empty, like you are just an ember barely smoking. And yet we can be at peace knowing that Jesus declares He will never let the smoking flax flame out completely. As long as there is smoke, there can be fire. Fire for the Lord! It is Jesus who promises to rekindle your fire so that your light can shine bright again and not be hidden but rather be seen of all for His glory.

The prophet Elijah in his despairing could do nothing but cry out to God. It is in that moment the Lord met him and reassured him in a still, small voice that He was there for him. It is the same Lord and same promise to you, beloved servant of Christ. He will never leave you nor forsake you (Heb. 13:5). Jesus will always be our comfort, our restorer, our peace (Eph. 2:14).

May our Lord's peace be upon you and with you beloved servant of the most high. May your bruises be healed and restored, and may your flax burn brightly as you continue to serve and share His truth for His judgment.

THOUGHTS

_____

_____

_____

_____

_____

_____

PRAYER

_____

_____

_____

_____

_____

_____

DAY 63

"I'm going fishing." Simon Peter said to them.

—John 21:3 (CSB)

HERE WE FIND the disciples waiting after the death and resurrection of our Lord Jesus Christ. Matthew and Mark tell us Jesus had instructed them to wait for Him in the mountain region of Galilee. However, we find them here waiting near the beach in Galilee. Although disobedient to the Lord's instruction, we can understand and relate as their hearts and minds were greatly troubled. A week had passed, and there was no appearance of Jesus as promised. Having great expectations of the kingdom reign, instead they witnessed the trial and execution of the Lord in Jerusalem. Their hearts were crushed, and in fear they probably left the mountains to check out the lower regions of Galilee in case they missed something. The disciples were confused, unsure of what to do and what was to come. They greatly missed their Lord after three years being together in ministry almost on a daily basis—depending on His leading and directing, teaching and counseling. So they headed to familiar territory, the Sea of Galilee, where they once fished for a living. The disciples needed a reset in life and ministry, and not knowing what to do next, they did what they knew best. They went fishing.

For many of us as Christians, we have seasons in life when we need a reset. We don't know what's next or where to go. We may be stalled or stymied or just plain exhausted from life and have no idea what to do. The disciples found their reset in Jesus. Although they were experts in fishing, they caught nothing after being out all night. A familiar voice yelled from the beach to toss the net on the other side of the boat. Reluctantly they complied, and to their surprise they were hauling in more fish than they could handle. The blessing of waiting on Jesus by just continuing in what you know. Keep showing up, keep punching the clock, and on His timing the reset will happen. New mercies, new grace, new directions, new confidence will come when we are faithful to what we know and continue to press on to the high calling. Peter, in going fishing, probably was on the water reminiscing over his times with Jesus at sea: The rebuking of the storm. Walking on water. The feeding of the five thousand while overlooking the sea. Amazing things that happened in the presence of the Lord. "I go fishing."

The Covid-19 pandemic brought forth a great reset in the hearts and spirits of many Christians. Many went back to church or found a new church. Sadly, others left the church and have not come back. Those who were blessed in coming back or finding new churches were going back to what they knew, the rock of our salvation, which was so needed at such a confusing time. It was a reset of faith for many, but to what end? How many are back in churches, back to what they know but just sitting and waiting unwilling to toss the net of their hearts and faith to the other side of the boat? Are they stuck sitting in the pews or are their hearts and minds anticipating a new direction, new purpose, new call, new dedication in a reset of faith? Are we just hanging out on the beach or willing to put ourselves out there in faith and go fishing to see what the Lord is going to do?

Peter and the other disciples went back to what they knew, and their reset transformed them from fishermen to fishers of men. What are you anticipating of the Lord, friend? While the day is at hand let your great reset be His best. Perhaps now is the time to get up and go fishing. Enough waiting and just start doing what you already know and be willing to hear and do what our Lord says. Be willing to toss your net to the other side. Our faith journeys are never about what we intend to make of the Lord, but rather what He intends to make of us.

THOUGHTS

PRAYER

DAY 64

"Break up your fallow ground, For it is time to seek the LORD,
till he comes and rains righteousness on you."

—Hosea 10:12 (NKJV)

IF YOU HAVE ever suffered an injury to your body, you may have had to undergo physical therapy to help it heal. If so, you would know to move forward in the healing process there is the painful messaging of the injured area over numerous sessions to break up the scar tissue to rebuild anew. As they say, "no pain, no gain."

Our passage today speaks to such a healing process but dealing with the scar tissue of hardened hearts and lives. The literal definition of *fallow ground* is the land that is left unseeded during a growing season which then becomes hard and impossible to bear the fruits of harvest. To produce fruit, the fallow ground will need to be broken up, cultivated, messaged, so to speak, to prepare the land to be seeded. The picture applies to humans who have hardened hearts and lives that need to be broken up and cultivated, messaged, in order for seeds of righteousness and truth to be sown and received so as to take root for God's blessings and works to flow from hearts and lives.

The first half of our verse speaks to sowing in righteousness. The idea is to let the seeds you sow be free and right and always of God's best. In doing so one will reap the blessings of God's mercy and bring forth much faith with an abundance of harvest to the glory of God. However, before such blessings and harvest can be attained, the grounds of our hearts and lives must be in a right place for God to use. The fallow ground must be broken up. The removal of hardness and prideful attitudes that can attach to oneself, religious practices, power and positions. Breaking up of the hardness of heart and negative issues of life requires self-reflection, repentance, surrender, commitment, and dedication to the Lord, and trusting in Him.

The passage concludes: "for it is time to seek the LORD." The Bible says, "seek the LORD while He may be found, Call on Him while He is near (Isa. 55:6 NKJV). The time is now for getting the soil of your heart right with God. There will be a time soon when it is too late to get the seed into the ground and into the field of your heart, and you will be unable to plant, let alone reap a harvest. One can only reap what they sow. Is it your time to break up the fallow ground of your heart? It may be painful in the short term, but what a glorious blessing that will come eternally. Remember, "no pain, no gain."

THOUGHTS

_____

_____

_____

_____

_____

_____

_____

PRAYER

_____

_____

_____

_____

_____

_____

_____

DAY 65

*"You are the salt of the earth. . . . You are the light
that shines for the world to see."*

—Matthew 5:13, 14 (ERV)

IN TODAY'S ECONOMY we hear of people making a living based on their on-line presence. They are called "influencers," and they pitch and create on-line content that is monetized based on the number of people who subscribe and follow them across various modes of social media. In today's passage we are reminded that, as Christians, we are called to be influencers in this world. It can be through social media platforms, but, as in our Lord's day, for most of us our influence is in the way we live our lives locally. As seen in our Jerusalems and Judeas as salt and light in this world.

In our Lord's day salt was used as a purifier, an antiseptic to heal wounds. Salt was also used as a preservative for meats and fish as there was no refrigeration in the day. Jesus is telling you believer that you are salt in this world as an agent of healing for wounded souls. You bring comfort to the broken and broken hearted with word and action, pointing people to the love of God. As preserving agents, Jesus is telling believers we are the ones to keep God's truth alive and relevant in this world. We are to stand boldly for the truth (Eph. 6:9), and we are not ashamed of the gospel of Jesus Christ (Rom. 1:16). A third aspect of salt that applies to our responsibility as world influencers for Christ is the natural effect salt has in a person when consumed. It makes one thirsty. Our influence should make people thirst for Christ and the love of God. Through everyday living and activity, how we handle the ups and downs of life should make people desire what we have in a true relationship with God through our Lord Jesus Christ.

So the question to you is what influence does your salt have in the world around you? In Matthew 5:13 Jesus warns of one's saltiness (influence) becoming unsalty or useless. It is good for nothing and thrown on paths to kill and destroy any vegetation and growth only to be trampled underfoot. The implication is that if one does not use one's gifts and privilege in the Lord as His people to influence others and glorify God, then we have lost our saltiness and are useless to God. We lack any purifying or preserving influence, and God forbid our actions and words leave people wanting nothing to do with the grace and knowledge of the Lord. Many churches today have lost their saltiness. We too as individuals can lose our saltiness and influence for Christ in the world. One can be backslidden, bitter, angry, jealous, prideful, all actions that can cause one to lose saltiness. It has been said that no one cares to hear what you have to say until they see or know that you actually care. So profound and so true. Is your influence in the world an outflow of God's love? Is your salt sprinkled in the world from the heart or tossed ineffectively from the flesh?

Jesus says we are the light of the world. Therefore, it is our duty to influence the world. As He was the light when on earth, Christians are now the light. We are His representatives pointing people to the love of God and shining brightly to show the way back home to fallen brethren. Light is seen not heard. Light dispels darkness. Light is not to be hidden. As light, our Christian influence is to be lived out openly for all to see and not in secret. Do people in your neighborhood, work, and places of community know you are a Christian? A light for the Lord? If so, are you having an influence in their lives?

Dearly beloved, get out there and shine brightly. Be a godly influence in your Jerusalem, starting in your home. Be an influence to your neighbors and neighborhood. Shine in your Judea, your workplace, and your community. And let the Lord lead you to the uttermost parts of the world in missionary work either by giving or going. Blind them with your love light, and let your salt of influence be forever salty.

In Jesus's name. Amen.

THOUGHTS

PRAYER

DAY 66

"Father, forgive them. They don't know what they are doing."

—Luke 23:24 (ERV)

"FATHER, FORGIVE THEM." Many scholars believe Jesus may have uttered these words the moment the iron pegs were being pounded through His hands and feet as He was being nailed to the cross. Our Lord's words speak to God's heart of mercy as Jesus asks His Father to forgive the Roman guards, and perhaps others on the scene, for their actions.

As I pray and agonize over the world and all the chaos, I can't help but be at peace. A smile even comes upon me because I know my Lord is interceding for all the unrighteousness going on, all the lawbreakers, and all the misguided ignorance of people as He did for those at His crucifixion, and as He did for me some years ago when I was one of the ignorant to His truth. The one who died for you is risen and at the right hand of God interceding for you (Rom. 8:34). We all have an advocate with God—Jesus Christ the righteous one (1 John 2:1). And it is Jesus who is able to save those who come to God through Him as He lives to intercede for them (Heb. 7:25). Praise the Lord! What hope it gives; what glory it shows.

When things feel hopeless, that is when true hope has victory. Jeremiah, the weeping prophet, continuously warned God's people of impending judgment, but his despair came from a place of hope that Judah might actually repent and be forgiven and saved. His hope was in knowing nothing is beyond God's reach, even the restoration and salvation of the wicked, let alone the ignorant. God said to Jeremiah: They will be my people, and I will be their God" (Jer. 32:38 CSB).

Beloved of God, as you look around and see all the crazy, the wrong, the moral decay, the wicked having their way, and too much ignorance, do not despair for God sees it all. That is our hope. God is still on the throne, and Jesus is there interceding. As God forgave the Roman soldiers, He forgave a wretch like me—and can forgive anyone. Even you, if you give your heart to Him. Ask to be forgiven, turn from the sinful ways of the present, be saved, and live for Him. In Jesus's name.

THOUGHTS

_____

_____

_____

_____

_____

_____

PRAYER

_____

_____

_____

_____

_____

_____

DAY 67

"I can do all things through Christ who strengthens me."

—Philippians 4:13 (NKJV)

OUR VERSE TODAY is well known for its great promise to the believer in Christ. However, it is often a misunderstood promise in that whatever one would want, need, desire, they can just "name it and claim it," or "blab it and grab it" and its yours to be had. The problem is when nothing happens, the claim is unfulfilled and there is nothing for one to grab. Taken in context this verse is much more glorious.

Paul's promise in the Lord is shared from personal experience not emotion. Paul in speaking knows firsthand that in whatever circumstance he finds himself he has learned to be content because he is strengthened by the Lord in all things. Paul learned how to make do with little and knows how to cherish and honor the Lord when blessed with a lot. Paul declares in either state, having little or having a lot, being well fed or hungry, having everything he needs or having nothing, he has learned to be content.

I recall when my wife and I felt led to step out in faith and for me to enroll in my local church's school of ministry. It was a struggle as my efforts were on school and not my livelihood. We came close to losing our home twice, but we did not waiver and were content with God's plan, whatever it looked like. He provided. Another time when we were new believers, we took on a fast and decided to extend it for a month by only drinking water and with protein powder once a day. After three days I woke up in the middle of the night famished and going crazy in hunger. I found myself hurrying to the refrigerator and opening the door. I grabbed a bowl of grapes. Eating one was pure joy! Then the second was like heaven! And then after the third grape my tummy and mind were completely content. We continued with our fasting program, and I did not eat another piece of food. The Lord strengthened me in weakness, and I learned contentment through an experience I lean on to this day.

So remember beloved, "you can do all things" is not a promise for more money or for a husband or wife or to have more faith or to satisfy an emotional want or need. Rather, our promise from Paul is that as you grow in the grace and knowledge of the Lord through life, He promises to strengthen you along the way in good times and bad times, in health and in sickness, in abundance and in leanness, in all things. It is so that you learn to be content no matter the circumstances in your walk with Him. "But godliness with contentment is great gain. For we brought nothing into this world, and we can take nothing out. (1 Tim. 6:6–7 CSB).

THOUGHTS

_____

_____

_____

_____

_____

_____

PRAYER

_____

_____

_____

_____

_____

_____

DAY 68

"Let me now go to the field, and glean ears of corn."

—Ruth 2:2 (BRG)

THE BOOK OF Ruth is set in the dark days of Judges when there was no king and everybody did what was right in their own eyes but was wicked in the eyes of God. God has made provision for Ruth and her mother in-law, Naomi. The law, as spelled out in the book of Leviticus (19:10) said that the foreigner, the widow, and the orphan, of which Ruth is all three, were allowed to go into the fields of the land and glean from the fields. In other words, the farmers were to leave the grain that fell on the ground for the poor to pick up. Faithfulness in a promise from God.

Our great and amazing God knows the beginning and the end. And in that end God's will and purposes shall be accomplished and completed with His own. It is God who works all things after the counsel of His own will (Eph. 1:11). Such is always the promise and faithfulness of God. It is in that character of love for us we are instructed to come and glean from the goodness and promises of God. Come and taste. God promises to restore what the locusts have stolen and to redeem what is lost. A bruised reed He shall never break, and a smoking flax He shall not quench. What God starts He finishes (Phil. 1:6). After waiting patiently, Abraham received what was promised (Heb. 6:15).

Precious Naomi, from the beginning of the book of Ruth, is seen as hopeless and empty, but by the end of the book she is restored in hope and full of joy. Ruth, a picture of faith and trust throughout the book, chose to stay near to God even in all her suffering and hardship. She chose to labor in trust, and it led her to a blessed rest. In the end her redemption was complete in all of God's glory.

Dearest beloved of God, His purposes and promises never fail. Keep laboring and keep gleaning after His glory as peace and rest will come.

THOUGHTS

_____

_____

_____

_____

_____

_____

PRAYER

_____

_____

_____

_____

_____

_____

DAY 69

"Take heed what you hear . . . .
Take heed therefore how you hear."

—Mark 4:24 & Luke 8:18 (NKJV)

MARK AND LUKE both share our Lord's words "take heed." Taking heed means "to listen," "to pay attention to" something, and "to be careful" about it. It is a warning to be heard and acted upon. In our passages the something is the Word of God. Jesus is saying there is a responsibility and accountability to those who hear the truth. Jesus has been teaching in parables. The word *parable* means "to cast alongside." In other words, it is a story that comes alongside a truth to shed light and understanding. Our Lord is teaching truths by sharing familiar stories that are also true. In context of both our passages Jesus is teaching the parables of the sower and light, and in both He is encouraging us to pay attention to what you hear and how you hear.

To the person who hears the Word of God, there is an obligation to understand the Word of God. To understand the Word of God means that the hearer is obligated to act upon the Word of God and to share the Word of God. To all who hear we are to become sowers of the Word and sharers of its light. We are to be scatterers of the seed, God's Word, sowing truth into the lives of others, and we are to shine the light of truth onto others so they may see God's Word. Light begets light, and wisdom begets wisdom. One who hears and responds to truth receives more truth; one who hears truth and does not respond will lose truth.

Take heed dearest beloved of God, all you who hear and pay attention have come out from the dark tunnel of sin into the light of God's grace. Be faithful to share with others what He has done for you. Faith comes by hearing and hearing by the Word of God (Rom. 10:17). Take heed the Word of God falls on good soil in your heart that fruit may come forth in abundance and your faith becomes greater, and stronger and that your light becomes brighter and brighter. Take heed you do not let what you hear go by the wayside of not responding to God's Word or that you hide what you hear and keep it a secret.

THOUGHTS

_____

_____

_____

_____

_____

_____

PRAYER

_____

_____

_____

_____

_____

_____

_____

DAY 70

*"Bless the L*ORD*, O my soul; and all that is within me,*
bless His holy name . . . . and forget not all His benefits."

—Psalm 103:1–2 (NKJV)

PSALM 103 FROM King David is a beautiful call to thanksgiving toward the Lord our God. It is a vivid reminder that we serve a good God. A God who loves us and adores us and saves us from our sinful selves.

The psalm begins with the word *bless*. It is the Hebrew word *barak*, which means "an act of adoration" and the root Hebrew word from which it comes suggests adoration from a place of kneeling. David is reminding us of our position when we praise and worship God. It is not necessarily in the literal sense of being on our knees, although that is not a bad place to be to get right with God. David is speaking to our attitudes attached to our worship and adoration to God. Our attitudes should be from a place of humility.

Humility is at the heart of all adoration and is essentially an expression of thankfulness. For the believer, it is our thankfulness to God. The opposite of humility is pride, which is what blinds one from recognizing all the goodness and awesome works of God in our lives. The Bible tells us the Lord hears the desires of the humble and strengthens their hearts (Ps. 10:17). The humble will have joy after joy in the Lord (Isa. 29:19). They will eat and be satisfied; those with humility seek the Lord and will praise Him (Ps. 22:26). The Bible tells us humility results in spiritual wealth, honor, and life (Prov. 22:4). So it is in humility that we are to bless the Lord. We worship and pour out our adoration for and to the one who saves us and loves us because we are so thankful.

Our passage also exhorts us to express our worship and thankful attitudes toward God with our soul and not just our lips. We are to be thankful with our entire being, spirit and body, heart and mind, all joining together to praise the holy name of Jehovah our Lord. Notice the poignant reminder: "forget not all His benefits." Thankfulness is born out of humility, and it is one's attitude of thanksgiving and thankfulness that breaks down and breaks through the barriers of self, allowing one to see the benefits of the Lord. The psalmist goes on to describe some of these benefits, how it is the Lord God who saves us from eternal death as He forgives us of our sins. He heals us from disease and redeems us from self-destruction. He crowns us with love and compassion and satisfies our passions and desires. He metes out righteousness and true justice for our benefit. He promises and fulfills His promises. All benefits from a loving relationship with a loving God. David says *don't forget!*

So beloved of God, my prayer for all of us is to feast on the Lord's love and express our love for Him in great worship and adoration for what He has done, is doing, and will do in our lives, in Jesus's name. Amen.

THOUGHTS

_____

_____

_____

_____

_____

_____

_____

PRAYER

_____

_____

_____

_____

_____

_____

DAY 71

"But there is hope for whoever is jointed with all the living,
since a live dog is better than a dead lion."

—Ecclesiastes 9:4 (CSB)

ARE YOU PASSIONATE about the Lord? Do you wake up every day anticipating great things to come of the day from the Lord? If you said yes, "even when we were dead in trespasses, [God] made us alive together with Christ (by grace you are saved)" (Eph. 2:5 NKJV).

Hope in Christ should be infectious. Nonbelievers should be attracted to the hope that is in us. Our family has two wonderful, passionate, enthusiastic, ecstatically joyful dogs who love their life. Anna and Elianna bring as much joy to our lives as they express in their lives. Joy is always infectious. Such is the point of our passage as it speaks to the fervor, passion, hope, and joy of life seen in a living dog. Years ago, I had the privilege of visiting the ministry field in Bogota, Columbia. As we weaved our way from the vast city to the low-lying mountainside populous, we would come into areas where there would be packs of dogs. Some ten to twenty of them, endlessly scavenging for morsels of food, always on the run to their next adventure. They never seemed angry or desperate, but rather they were joyfully going about their life. I asked our guide what was up with all the stray dogs. He smiled and told me that each of them has a home and that this was just their daily routine.

In contrast to the living dog is the lifelessness and hopelessness of the dead lion. With all its greatness, power and might, the king of the jungle, the lion, spends most of its time lying around sleeping. Where is the joy and enthusiasm for life? One day they are on the hunt for life, the next just basking in their own revelry. Dead enthusiasm. Dead passion for life. As one scholar shared about this passage, it is likened to when Christ came into Jerusalem for His passion week. The men and women were shouting, "Hosanna, King of the Jews!" at the beginning, but in the end those dead lions were crying, "Crucify Him!"

For the Christian there is no option other than to be joyful and enthusiastic in and for life. You are a beloved child of God. You are saved for eternity in heaven! Your name is written in the Lamb's book of life! Anything less than joy and passion for life speaks to a lack of spiritual consecration and discipline as a follower of Christ. As the bride of Christ, we are representatives of joy and hope in this world. We are to be among the living; we are to be among other Christians manifesting optimism and enthusiasm for Christ. We are not dead like the sleepy lion, but rather we are alive in Christ as a joyful, excited, and content dog. Let your hope be seen in your living.

THOUGHTS

PRAYER

DAY 72

*"So I beg you, brothers and sisters, because of the great mercy
God has shown us, offer your lives as a living sacrifice to him—
an offering that is only for God and pleasing to him.
Considering what he has done, it is only right that
you should worship him in this way."*

—Romans 12:1 (CSB)

"I BEG YOU" Paul writes. Look at all God has done for me!
For you! He has freely given us salvation, redemption, reconciliation, and deliverance from the power of sin. He has given us His
tender mercies, His grace of blessings, His unconditional love
and forgiveness, and His overwhelming kindness in our lives.
How could one not offer themselves as a living sacrifice to God?
How could one not want to present themselves as an offering of
godly conduct for all He has done?

Our passage today speaks to a sacrifice ceremonially offered
as part of our worship to God. The offering as such would be
considered by God to be holy and acceptable and set apart
entirely for God's use. Whether it be money, gifts, or time, an
offering is voluntary. Paul is telling the reader to present, or in
this case yield, one's physical body voluntarily as an offering to
God, rendering one's body holy and acceptable and set apart
from the world to be used by God. It is quite a heavy statement
by Paul.

I believe Paul may be summarizing our Lord's words when
Jesus says, "If anyone would come after me, let him deny himself"
(Matt. 16:24 ESV). The idea our Lord is conveying is to yield
oneself. Yield to God's complete control over yourself—body,
mind, and soul. Yielding ourselves as living sacrifices to God's
will and purpose. Jesus goes on to say to take up your cross. In
other words, be willing to endure the shame and suffering and

persecution as a living sacrifice to God. Every Christian knows we are not of this world and that struggles will come, but are we willing to endure through it all as Christ did for us? Jesus concludes by telling them, to follow Him. A living sacrifice for God is to yield one's life to God and in doing so you are to live as Christ lived, following His lead in life. It is to live your life always in the godly virtues of faith, hope, and love. Such is the best of our living and active worship to God as living sacrifices. Paul says it's only right to act this way for all He has done. I like the New King James Version that states we should offer our lives as a living sacrifice to God as it is our reasonable service to God. For all He has done it is reasonable to live as an offering to God. It is not up for theological debate, but rather living a life holy and acceptable to God set apart for His will and purpose is the highest form of worship to God.

Our bodies are temples for the Holy Spirit (1 Cor. 6:19) and thus our bodies are the instruments God uses to reach the world for His truth.

Therefore, beloved of God, choose this day and every day to present and yield your body as a living sacrifice, an offering for God's use. Paul tells the Ephesians to "pay careful attention to how you walk—not as unwise people but as wise—making the most of the time, because the days are evil. So don't be foolish, but understand what the Lord's will is" (Eph. 5:15–17 CSB). In death, Jesus yielded His body to the cross so that you could freely yield your body in life to Him and His way. This is our reasonable worship to God.

THOUGHTS

_____

_____

_____

_____

_____

_____

_____

PRAYER

_____

_____

_____

_____

_____

_____

_____

DAY 73

"Because of these things, the Lord God says. 'I will put a rock—
a cornerstone—in the ground in Zion. This will be a very precious
stone. Everything will be built on this very important rock.
Anyone who trusts in this rock will not be disappointed.'"

—Isaiah 28:16 (ERV)

OUR VERSE TODAY speaks to the time when Israel's leaders were making political treaties and deals, relying on secular alliances to put their trust in for security and safety rather than trusting in God. God responds by declaring to the Israelites there is a firm foundation that will be in Zion. A precious stone pointing metaphorically to the coming Messiah as the true foundation of faith for God's people. "The Lord is my rock, and my fortress, and my deliverer; my God, my strength, in whom I will trust, my buckler, and the horn of my salvation, and my high tower." (Ps. 18:2 BRG)

It is the believer's trust in the true and living God as our rock that will bring calmness in the storms, provide peace in the chaos, and bring wisdom, strength, discernment, and comfort in tumultuous times. One who depends on God and not humans or human wisdom will lead to long-term stability in life and in nations. The stone which the builders rejected (Jesus Christ) is the chief cornerstone to those of the Christian faith.

God's nature is the same yesterday, today, and forever, and the fullness of God's nature is in Christ Jesus (Col. 2:9). Christ is the radiance of God's glory and the exact expression of God's nature, sustaining all things by His powerful word (Heb. 1:3). His nature is unchanged, and His promises are for you, believer, in good times and in bad times. His love endures forever. Build your life on His rock, the firm foundation of Christ, and you will not be moved or staggered or destroyed in times of crisis. You will be just fine in Christ Jesus.

THOUGHTS

_____

_____

_____

_____

_____

_____

PRAYER

_____

_____

_____

_____

_____

_____

DAY 74

"That the trial of your faith, being much more precious
than of gold that perisheth, though it be tried with fire,
might be found unto praise and honour and glory
at the appearing of Jesus Christ."

—1 Peter 1:7 (KJV)

AS I WRITE this devotional my heart breaks and my spirit is weak from witnessing the horror of wildfires that have decimated Los Angeles county recently. Thank God my family and I are not directly in the line of the fires, but it is so heartbreaking to hear of the twenty-four lives (and counting) that have perished in the fires—to see the destruction of more than ten thousand homes, hundreds of businesses going up in flames, and to see the aftermath of long-standing neighborhoods completely destroyed displacing some 130,000 residents. My heart aches for the men, women, children, and families who fled for their lives and for some with nothing but the clothes they were wearing. So many memories for me growing up. The picturesque views driving Pacific Coast Highway in Malibu where I once worked in a local restaurant and learned to surf is now littered with heaps of burned down homes and businesses. I am truly humbled by so many who have lost everything but testify of being grateful for their lives and the lives of their family members. This tragedy has reminded me through the Spirit of God that in the end all that really matters in life are the relationships you have with each other and most important the relationship one has with God.

The apostle speaks of life that must persevere to the end (1 Pet. 1:7). No matter where our journey in this world takes us, or the trials that test us, we want to show up on the day of eternal destiny in good standing with God. Peter exhorts us on the value of faith and how our faith will be tested in life to prove that it is genuine. He provides a vivid picture of the transformation people have when they have a genuine encounter with the living God. As fire refines gold the dross rises to the top to be removed. In the same way trials in life exposes the dross of sin so that we may confess it and bring one back into a redemptive and pure and righteous standing with God. As the proverbs proclaims: "the refining pot is for silver and the furnace for gold, But the LORD is the tester of hearts" (Prov. 17:3 NKJV).

As horrific as the California fires have been, I have seen the Lord at work: Neighbors loving neighbors like never before. People banning together sharing of goods and comforting one another. A wave of humility has sprung up, as people's hearts have been tested and refined understanding what is truly valuable in life. It has forced so many to check their faith. To lean on God for comfort and peace in the midst of such a storm. To consider one's ways and priorities. To draw on the truth of Paul's words to the Philippians: "whatever is true, whatever is honorable, whatever is just, whatever is pure, whatever is lovely, whatever is commendable—if there is any moral excellence and if there is anything praiseworthy—dwell on these things" (Phil. 4:8 CSB).

As with all tragedies, we should pray for those who lost loved ones. Pray for those who lost so much and must start rebuilding their lives again. Pray for the first responders who tirelessly sacrifice themselves. And please pray that the grace of the Lord will be poured out on these communities and people, that a great awakening and great refining of hearts would take place so that they may embrace a pure and righteous relationship with God and begin living life with an eternal perspective and hearts desiring to draw near to God. Pray that the people suffering would have a faith refined to outwardly express praise, glory, and honor in a genuine relationship with Jesus Christ our Lord. "Blessed are those who mourn, for they shall be comforted . . . . Blessed are the pure in heart: for they shall see God" (Matt. 5:4, 8 KJV).

THOUGHTS

_____

_____

_____

_____

_____

_____

PRAYER

_____

_____

_____

_____

_____

_____

DAY 75

"As a lion or young lion growls over its prey when an band of shepherds is called out against it, and it is not terrified by their shouting or subdued by their noise, so the LORD of armies will come down to fight on Mount Zion and on its hill. Like hovering birds, so the LORD of armies will protect Jerusalem; by protecting it, he will rescue it; by passing over it, he will deliver it."

—Isaiah 31:4–5 (CSB)

AS FALLEN PEOPLE, we are inclined to put our trust in other people and worldly processes rather than trusting and persevering in God over the matters of life. Our verse of the day speaks to our inclination to not trust God. Nevertheless, He remains passionate and has the resolve over His people in protecting and preserving them.

Isaiah 31 is a rebuke of those who put their trust in the Egyptians and the folly in so doing as it is the Lord who is their power and protector. It is the Lord who is unchangeable and will preserve. Like a lion whose power, passion, and determination never to lose grip of its prey, so is our Lord's power, passion, and determination to never lose grip of His people. Have you ever tried to take away a snack from a pet dog? Don't. The Bible promises no enemy can snatch God's people from His eternal hand (John 10:29).

Like a hovering flock of birds, the Lord's care and compassion for His people is as that of birds defending their young. My wife loves gardening and has created several beautiful flower baskets around our yard. At times the birds create nests for their young in a basket. To keep the flowers from dying the baskets must still be watered but very carefully so as not to disturb the nest and the eggs. As careful as we are in watering, it does not stop the mother and father of the eggs from dive-bombing near our heads to let us know their displeasure. As the Bible also promises, God is for us and His people, and nothing will be allowed to come against us (Rom 8:31).

Isaiah reminds those who are of God and are not trusting in God in some situation to repent and turn back to trusting God. His love will never let go. Return to Him, persevere in Him. His love and care is unrelenting and will always triumph over the ways of the world for God's glory. He fights and cares for you and it's always best to give it to Him.

THOUGHTS

PRAYER

DAY 76

"If thou faint in the day of adversity, thy strength is small"

—Proverbs 24:10 (KJV)

ADVERSITY COMES IN the forms of difficulty, hardships, distress, misfortune, calamity, and unfavorable events. For the Christian, adversity is the measuring stick by which you stand and serve God. If someone does nothing during times of adversity, their faith will be limited and the strength to stand tall in life and serve God will be weak.

I was recently reminded of the power of overcoming adversity while watching a documentary series *Vietnam; The War That Changed America*. The series depicts video footage of first-person accounts of America's longest and arguably most disastrous foreign war in terms of the adversity faced by our soldiers who served in the war. The documentary depicts the adversities the soldiers endured from the North and South Vietnamese armies as well. The stories are intense and horrific, and include the terrible struggles American soldiers faced returning home to a divided America.

I found myself often getting emotional watching the war footage and reunions years later. There was a soldier who was reunited with the helicopter pilot who rescued him at great risk. A father who was deployed when his daughter was four weeks old and after seven years as a prisoner of war and presumed dead was reunited with his wife and daughter, who are all still together this day. Nurses are shown reuniting with the soldiers they saved. Soldiers are reunited with other soldiers with whom they fought side by side but never knew what happened to each other. The tears were everywhere.

Emotion caught the best of me as the Vietnam war was personal. I certainly did not experience the same adversity as those who served and the families affected by their service, but I do recall as a child my parents arguing over my brother who was just a few months away from the draft lottery before it ended. My father was a reservist in the Navy during the Korean War and insisted my brother serve if called upon, but with the horrors seen on the news every night my mother wanted him to go to Canada rather than be subject to the atrocities going on in the war. I also remember the soldiers coming home in our small town in California. They did not receive a hero's welcome.

A few years later in high school, while working at a custom van conversion shop, we would be visited by a photographer from *Van* magazine who became a friend of the shop as he photographed our projects for publication. He always wore his army jacket, and I knew he was a Vietnam war veteran. One day over lunch in the shop I asked him about his experience. He said it was a living hell, and he went on to tell me that as a gunner on a helicopter they had to rescue a platoon one day. As they flew into the clearing the men from the platoon came running out of the jungle only to be mowed down by gunfire one after another. He said they were only able to rescue two men from the slaughter. He had tears in his eyes telling the story, and it helped me understand why he was always low key and such a quiet person. His eyes even seemed hollow to me as he no doubt carried around a deep hurt over his service in the war. His story stuck with me, and I so wish I had been a born-again believer back then so I could share with him the love and hope of Jesus Christ who gives strength to the brokenhearted, who heals us, and makes us overcomers.

As I was off to college and moved on with life, I don't know what happened to my photographer friend, but I do know that adversity will afflict everyone in life at some time. But God will give us love and hope in the midst of our adversities (Ps. 34:19). As believers we can become stronger in character through adversity (James 1:2–4). We can overcome with the spiritual disciplines of Scripture reading and study, prayer, and fellowship with like-minded Christians. We can be hopeful knowing that God is always faithful. To anyone facing unsurmountable adversity, find comfort in the words from Psalm 42:11 (CSB): "Why, my soul, are you so dejected? Why are you in such turmoil? Put your hope in God, for I will still praise Him, my Savior, and my God."

Blessed are those who overcome adversity with truth, suffering with love, and endure difficulty with hope. In Jesus's name. Amen.

THOUGHTS

_____

_____

_____

_____

_____

_____

PRAYER

_____

_____

_____

_____

_____

_____

DAY 77

*"To everything there is a season, and a time
to every purpose under heaven"*

—Ecclesiastes 3:1 (NKJV)

OUR VERSE FOR today speaks to seasons of life and goes on to list some of those seasons. We are born, we die, we sow, we harvest. There is killing; there is healing. Life breaks down; we build life up again. We weep, we laugh, we mourn, we dance, we throw away the past. We gather for the future, we embrace matters, we hold off on matters. We win, we lose, we gain. We throw away, we shred, we sew. There are times of silence; there are times to speak. We love, we hate, we war, and we live in peace (Eccl. 3:2–8).

The writer King Solomon, a very wise man, asks the question What profit does one gain from all the struggles of life? (v. 9). Or another way it can be said: What is to gain from the all the seasons of life one goes through? King Solomon recognizes there are seasons in life that can be good, bad, ugly, blessed, wanting, joyful, sorrowful, and so on. The king is also telling the reader the most important thing is that God is in control and always at work in our lives through all seasons. The prophet Jeremiah declares that God has good plans for His people. Plans to prosper oneself and not bring harm. Plans to give each of His people a hope and a future (Jer. 29:11). God is always at work in His children's lives. The apostle Paul shares this same sentiment in his letter to the Romans when he writes: "all things work together for the good of those who love God, who are called according to his purpose" (Rom. 8:28 CSB).

Life is all about seasons. We are either coming out of a season, in the midst of a season, or going into a season, and includes seasons of rest. Seasons come and go. No season lasts forever.

Whatever season you are in know that God is in control and will take you through the season for His good purpose. We are to submit and enjoy the ride (as best we can).

Thirteen years ago the Lord called me and my family from the northeast to move back to California. It would become a new season of ministry. My wife was certain I would land in a blessed new position and believed it would take six months, so I should enjoy my season of rest from twelve years of church planting and being a vocational pastor and gain strength for the next season. It did take six months before a new season began, and of course I was too anxious and missed the blessed season of rest the Lord provided. I learned a lesson though. More recently, the Lord has led me to step out in another venture in faith for a new season of life. Because of my age some have concluded that I am stepping into retirement and the sunset of life. But as I told a friend, it is not a sunset I am stepping into but rather a sunrise, into a new season in life and ministry, and I can't wait to see what the Lord has in store.

THOUGHTS

_____

_____

_____

_____

_____

_____

PRAYER

_____

_____

_____

_____

_____

_____

DAY 78

"So then Jesus said plainly, Lazarus is dead. And I am glad
I was not there. I am happy for you because now you
will believe in me. We will go to him now."

—John 11:14–15 (ERV)

THE APOSTLE JOHN tells the account of Lazarus being raised
from the dead (John 11:1–44). Lazarus was the brother of Mary
and Martha and a dear friend of Jesus. He had become ill, and
word was sent to Jesus who was only a few miles away to come
and help. But Jesus delayed His coming and Lazarus died.

The account of Lazarus is so powerful not only in the miracle
of the resurrection, but in application as it speaks to God's plan,
which is always better than our plan, and to God's purpose,
which is always best over our purpose. The followers of Jesus are
expecting the Lord to come and heal Lazarus from his illness.
But Jesus delayed His arrival four days. To make everyone know
the reality of the moment, the Lord says Lazarus is dead. Not sick
but dead. I love the King James Version, which tells us once Jesus
had arrived, the body of Lazarus "stinketh." The body was full of
decay and rotting away. Upon Jesus arrival, Martha and Mary
were distraught and grieving and quite dismayed at the Lord's
delay. Their expectations of God in this circumstance were not
met. Martha's faith shined brightly in her confidence that in the
end Lazarus will be resurrected unto life, but in that moment,
death was not expected.

Beloved, in the trials and tests of life we often tend not to
see God as the author and finisher of our plans. How we forget
that God's plan is always better. After grieving over Lazarus's
death, along with Martha and Mary and the other mourners,
Jesus declared: "Remember what I told you? I said that if you
believed, you would see the Lord's divine greatness. So they

moved the stone away from the entrance. Then Jesus looked up and said, 'Father, I thank you that you heard me. I know that you always hear me. But I said these things because of the people here around me. I want them to believe that you sent me.' After Jesus said this He called with a loud voice, 'Lazarus, come out!'" (John 11:40–43 CSB).

I like to think that as part of God's divine greatness when the stone was rolled away from the grave there was a horrendous stench of death that blew away the people. And then out walks Lazarus for effect. This account speaks to how we so often want our dark circumstances to be resolved our way. We have certain expectations, but God's plan is greater, and His process is best. He sees the greater healing, the greater provision. He knows when we are beaten and bruised and feeling like we are left for dead. He sees it, knows it all, and works it all for the good of those who love Him (Rom. 8:28). He delayed His coming for a greater purpose. People needed to believe. I think of the Lord today and His second coming and how it's delayed for more people to believe and to be saved. But He will come, and the greater purpose will bring this world to an end.

The people in the Lazarus account had an expectation. They knew the process through the healing of a blind man. How could the Lord delay and not save Lazarus? They wanted a resuscitation, but instead the Lord gave them a resurrection. All to the greater plan and process and purpose of God.

THOUGHTS

_____

_____

_____

_____

_____

_____

PRAYER

_____

_____

_____

_____

_____

_____

DAY 79

"The next night the Lord Jesus came and stood by Paul.
He said, "Be brave! You have told people in Jerusalem about me.
You must do the same in Rome."

—Acts 23:11 (ERV)

AT THE END of the book of Acts we find Paul on his way to Rome as a prisoner when the ship he is on encounters a great storm off the Island of Crete. Being battered and tossed by the storm for many days, throwing cargo overboard to lighten the ship and not capsize, having little food and water, all 276 souls aboard, including crew and prisoners, saw hope for survival fading. However, Paul stands among the men and exhorts them to be of good cheer and to have courage as all on board will survive (Acts 27:21). We recognize the confidence and boldness of Paul's declaration as a surety and we know he had been visited by the angel of God the night before who told Paul to not be afraid, for it was necessary for him to appear before Caesar in Rome, and God would graciously deliver all the men to safety. So Paul's declaration in the midst of a great storm, with seemingly no hope, tells everyone it's going to be okay, and they will survive.

I don't know about you, but when I face storms of life, I can find myself struggling to stand in confidence and boldness of my faith. My hope is not lost, but I am challenged in heart and mind not knowing what the outcome will be. But the fact remains to those who believe and walk in faith, the promise is that no matter the storms we face, everything will turn out for good of those who love Him (Rom. 8:28).

It bodes well to recognize Paul's confidence and boldness of faith is rooted in a prior experience from a past promise. Earlier Paul was perhaps in his darkest moment in ministry. In the deep pit of the prison after sharing his personal testimony of grace and salvation in and through Jesus Christ. His heart desired more than anything to get to Rome to share the good news with his fellow Romans. Yet all hope was seemingly lost. He felt it was the end of his service as he was facing sure death. It is here in Paul's darkest moment that the Lord Jesus appeared to him in that prison cell and promised, "be of good cheer, Paul; for as you have testified for Me in Jerusalem, so you must also bear witness at Rome" (Acts 23:11 NKJV). A promise made by our Lord. And a promise Paul did not forget.

We have to remember God's promises and the times in the past He delivered on those promises so that in the midst of our life storms we can stand boldly and confidently in our faith. Remember, God's thoughts and heart toward us is for peace and not evil, plans to prosper us and not harm us, plans to give us hope and a bright future (Jer. 29:11), and that He is our sun and shield, and gives grace and glory and no good thing will He withhold from them that walk uprightly (Ps. 84:11). "The Lord will always lead you, satisfy you in a parched land, and strengthen your bones. You will be like a watered garden and like a spring whose water never runs dry" (Is. 58:11 CSB). We must never forget our experiences when God brought that needed job, the necessary provision, a healing, blessings in our marriages and relationships, wisdom for a problem, and times of great joy and rejoicing in our service to God.

We know how it turned out for Paul. After fourteen days in the storm, seasick, starving, thirsting, Paul and all 276 men aboard the ship, after partaking in a communion service, cut anchor and let the ship run to shore. Hitting a sandbar, the ship broke apart, many swimming to shore, others used boards from the ship letting the waves take them to shore (this Californian rejoices seeing the invention of surfing!). Everyone reached the shore safely on the Island of Malta where they would rest from the stormy season in the Mediterranean Sea, and Paul prepared his heart to share the good news to his people as he would be delivered to Rome, fulfilling the promise made to him by the Lord (Acts 27:33–28).

The Lord's promises are the same yesterday, today, and forever. Whatever storms we face His thoughts do not change toward us. They are always good. So be of good cheer, believer! Remember the past experiences of His promises that did come true. Do not fear the storm you may be in, but rather stand boldly and confidently in your faith knowing it is going to be okay.

THOUGHTS

_____

_____

_____

_____

_____

_____

_____

PRAYER

_____

_____

_____

_____

_____

_____

Special
Devotions

DAY 80

"And that knowing the time, that now is high time to wake from sleep, for now is our salvation nearer than when we first believed. The night is nearly over, and the day is at hand; let us therefore discard the deeds of darkness and put on the armor of light. Let us walk with decency, as in the daytime: not in rioting or drunkenness, not in sexual impurity and promiscuity; not in quarreling and jealousy. But put on the Lord Jesus Christ and make no provision for the flesh to fulfill its desires."

—Romans 13:11-14

WAKE UP, WASH UP, & WISE UP

AFTER EXHORTING THE church in Rome to love one another, Paul goes on to passionately declare to the body of Christ that the time is now to *wake up, wash up,* and *wise up!* With the onslaught of persecution Paul believed the day of the Lord's return was at hand and closer than ever before. Reading the Bible makes it clear that the Lord's return is imminent for every generation. The difference between then and now is that the believer today has fulfilled prophecy that in prior centuries were allegorical or metaphorical. One can read today the prophecies of Matthew 24, Luke 21, Daniel, Revelation, Ezekiel 37 and 38, and others and literally see the signs spoken of Jesus and the prophets that have been met and are upon the world today. We live in times of a world order rising, tensions among nations are at epic levels, good is being called evil and evil is called good. Jesus warned that before His return "the love of many shall wax cold" (Matt. 24:12 BRG). The apostle Peter, writing for his generation, said that "the end of all things is at hand, therefore be alert and sober minded for prayer" (1 Pet. 4:7 CSB). Jesus, also speaking to the end times before His return, proclaimed "when you see these things happening, recognize the kingdom of God is near" (Luke 21:31 CSB).

I believe in my heart we are on the doorstep of our Lord's return and the call on Christians today now more than ever is to live with an attitude of looking up for His return. We are to live as if Jesus could descend at any moment, on any day. So what is the Christian to do? As Paul declares, we are to *wake up*! This is no time to slack off in your relationship and walk with the Lord. Cheap grace will not cut it when the Lord comes. We are to wake up, see the signs, and live with anticipation of the coming. The word for "sleep" in our passage in the Greek language is defined as "position" or "condition of inferiority." In other words, you don't want to be caught sleeping or caught off guard. The parable of the ten virgins is a great lesson on not missing out on the coming of the groom. We as believers are not to be caught clueless to the signs and conditions in the world. We want to be people of understanding. People of spiritual understanding of the times. We want to be as the two hundred men of the tribe of Issachar who were described as men that understood the times (1 Chron. 12:32). So wake up beloved of God and do as Jesus did and be busy about the Father's business. Especially as we see the day approaching.

After we wake up, it only follows that one should wash up. Paul is saying get busy and clean yourself up. Now is not the time as Christians to be about living a sinful lifestyle. Jesus told us people walk in darkness rather than the light because their deeds are evil, and they would rather not come to the light lest their evil deeds be exposed (John 3:19–20). Paul says to "discard the deeds of darkness" (Rom. 13:12 CSB). The idea is to cast off, throw them away, far away, not just set them aside for a moment or season but to get rid of them forever. Listen beloved, the degree of dirt and dark deeds is not the issue. All dirt and dark deeds need washing off. Christians are to be on good godly behavior. The dark world is watching you. If we walk in dishonesty, immorality, debauchery, division, and jealousy, then we cannot be used by God. Now is also the time to die to self. We are not to plant our minds in pity parties and self-indulgence. Your safe place is in godly relationships and the body of Christ. You, believer, are washed in the blood of Christ. Walk worthy today of such grace.

After declaring to wake up and wash up, Paul tells us to wise up. Do not make provisions for the flesh. Do not waste time messing with the temptations of the world. For Christians, to wise up really means to grow up in our faith. To get off the milk and onto the meat of God's word—and not just talk the talk but walk the walk. Stop feeding the flesh and get serious about feeding the spirit—not just in knowledge but in self-discipline and action to honor Christ all of our days. Be determined to obey God and submit to His truth. Walk wisely in the Spirit as we navigate the times. It may take carrying a heavy burden, but as Peter professes, we are to cast off our burdens, our cares, our anxieties and worry, our concerns and put them on Jesus because He cares for us (1 Pet. 5:7).

The apostle Paul lays down the challenge, beloved of God. It is time to *wake up*. We are to understand the times we live in as God's people, knowing the time for the Lord's return is near. We are to *wash up*. Clean up the darkness and filth in your life holding you back from God's best for you and your loved ones. And we are to *wise up*. Walk worthy of God's grace in this world and see it for what it is through a spiritual prism, always having a fervent desire to grow in the grace and knowledge of our Lord.

Jesus is coming soon!

THOUGHTS

PRAYER

DAY 81

"The LORD said to Gideon, "I will deliver you with the three hundred who lapped and hand the Midianites over to you. But everyone else is to go home."

—Judges 7:7 (CSB)

THE DOGS OF WAR

THIS IS AN amazing historical event recorded in the Bible. Gideon and his army of thirty-two thousand men are called into battle against 135,000 Midianites. His men are full of worry and anxiety and letting their feelings be known to Gideon. God tells those of Gideon's army who are fearful to go home (v. 3). Twenty-two thousand fighting men leave. The odds are now 6.1 to 1. But God wants to make sure His people know who can and who gets the glory for victory for this seemingly impossible battle. He just needs a few good men.

The remaining ten thousand of Gideon's army are ordered to the river to drink (v. 4). It is a test and those found drinking water with their tongues like a dog were three hundred and this is all the Lord required to go into battle against the 135,000. Many scholars suggest the men who bent down to drink the water from the riverbank showed a propensity to bow down as in the way of idol worship. It can also be a picture showing a lack of attention in bowing or bending as one would lose focus and awareness of what was going on around them. For the three hundred soldiers who drank using their hands to cup the water and lap it up like a dog, they could have been prostate as well, but the picture is more reflective of the Hebrew custom of worship in the day, not idol worship. They may have been standing as well after cupping the water, and regardless of either position, it shows a picture of attentiveness and awareness of their surroundings. These are the 300 God has chosen to go against 135,000. I call them God's Dogs of War. Outnumbered 450 to 1, the odds are crazy and impossible.

The Lord God will have victory regardless of any odds against Him, and in this scenario, we find victory is not complete without the obedience of the three hundred. God instructs Gideon to implore a crazy military strategy with the men holding torches and trumpets in their left hands and smashing jars with their right hands. The torches symbolize the truth of God's light and faithfulness to His everlasting Word. The trumpets are symbolic of standing against one's enemies and loudly proclaiming the truth of God. And God required the three hundred to be obedient. As crazy and difficult the odds were before them, the men stepped up. It is said the worth of a soldier is never known in times of peace, only in times of battle.

You and I are in a great battle today. It is a spiritual battle that is going on in the world as evil seems to be having its way more and more every day. Nevertheless, in the battles we know and trust we serve the same God as Gideon and his three hundred dogs of war. God's people are partakers of a righteous army that should know no weapon formed against them can win in the end, and it is our duty to be obedient soldiers that will stand and shout for God today, to hold up the light of His glorious truth and loudly declare it to a dying world. A pastor I highly admire, Chuck Swindoll, in his book *David* shares three points on the call of David to serve as one of God's mightiest warriors and king:

> *First*, God's solutions are often strange and simple . . . be open. Second, God's provisions are usually sudden and surprising . . . be ready. And third, God's selections are always sovereign and sure . . . be calm.[1]

---

[1] Charles R. Swindoll, *David: A Man of Passion and Destiny,* Bible Study Guide (Nashville: Thomas Nelson Publishers, 1997), 15.

Don't let people and warfare turn you back from your call. And I would just add: be obedient to God's call on your life.

As believer's we are all called into the spiritual battles set before us. The challenge is who of the thirty-two thousand will you aspire to be? Maybe times have griped you with fear, and you feel you need to stay on the sidelines. That may be okay in grace for a season, but God's best is to eventually stand and forge ahead. Discipline yourself to be reading God's Word to fortify and strengthen your spirit. Pray and pray often. Get in a church that faithfully teaches the full counsel of God's Word and serve in some capacity. Continue to press in not away, so when the call comes again you will be open, ready, calm, and obedient.

Perhaps you may not know it, but you are as one of the ninety-seven hundred not ready in spirit and faith to serve God. Your trust may be in a pastor, counselor, or friend rather than God. Maybe your heart trusts more in religion or the institution and traditions of religion rather than God. If this is you and your heart, you are missing out on God's best for you and will be sent home rather than be used for the glory of God. Such is a time for a faith check. Where does your help come from, and who do you really trust in to lead and guide your life? What are you truly willing to stand and shout for?

For me, and I pray for you, that you are as the three hundred, a mighty dog of war for God's army for such a time as this. I want to be standing and shouting for God's truth. Holding up the light of His truth, ever faithful to the Word of God. And ready to obey when called upon to surrender to His will not my will.

Let me leave you with the inspiring story from the Civil War. A young man who was a schoolteacher, a devout Christian, and a man given to the power of prayer, volunteered for the Union Army. Answering the call he quickly rose in rank. Major General Joshua Lawrence Chamberlin in 1863 led 386 men in the Battle of Gettysburg to defend the Union's left flank on a hill known as Little Round Top. Heavily outnumbered and having already endured six attacks from the Confederate Army, the seventh attack came with a fury. His men exhausted and low on ammunition, Chamberlin shouted "bayonets!" In obedience, his remaining men charged down the hill in such a loud and ferocious counterattack that the Confederate Army turned and retreated. Historians believe this act of heroism not only turned the momentum in the Union's favor to grab victory in the Battle of Gettysburg, but it also changed the course of the entire Civil War that led to the Union victory. Chamberlin and his embattled three hundred-plus dogs of war could have retreated to a safer place and given up the high ground to the enemy. Instead, in obedience and no matter the cost they strapped on their bayonets and ran into battle trusting in their leader, and God, for victory.

Beloved, now more than ever we are being called on as Christians to strap on our bayonets—our sword, the Word of God—and run into battle shinning and shouting about God's glory and truth. If not yet, you will be called for specific duty. You may be in between assignments. How will you answer when the call comes? We are to fight earnestly for the faith that was delivered to the saints once for all (Jude 3)

The Lord God needs more warriors to stand and serve today. Answer His call and be a part of the three hundred club, the mighty dogs of war.

THOUGHTS

_____

_____

_____

_____

_____

_____

_____

PRAYER

_____

_____

_____

_____

_____

_____

_____

DAY 82

"Now these three remain: faith, hope, and love—
but the greatest of these is love."

1 Corinthians 13:13 (CSB)

THE WAY OF LOVE

THE APOSTLE PAUL is writing to the Corinthian church, addressing problems they were undergoing (as all churches and organizations face), and he provides great wisdom and instruction to the fellowship of believers. In the previous chapter Paul taught on the gifts of the Holy Spirit and their applications to edify the body of Christ. In the next chapter Paul instructs on more specifics of each gift and how they bless the church not only in Corinth but all churches.

Nestled wonderfully between is the great chapter on love as applied to the church body. Chapter 12 ends with Paul imploring the believers to seek, desire, earnestly covet the best gifts. What are the best gifts? The best gifts for the body of Christ are the gifts that a church needs. Whether it be wisdom or knowledge, faith, healing, miracles, prophesy, discernment, or the gift of tongues; Paul is saying the best gift is the one needed for the moment and circumstances, but all are to be applied with the better way, the more excellent way—the way of *agape*.

Agape is the Greek word for love that is the divine love received in faith through the Holy Spirit. It is the love of God within a Christian that transcends emotion, feelings, and duty and is expressed as a sacrificial, unconditional, and unending action. The more excellent way.

In chapter 13 Paul begins by telling the body of Christ you can be blessed with spiritual gifts, but if one does not exercise the gifts in love—Agape love—such gifts will come across only as noise to the intended recipients. Spiritual gifts without love behind the purpose will miss the mark and fall short or completely miss the target all together. It's the idea behind Paul's exhortation that "love does no wrong to a neighbor. Love, therefore, is the fulfillment of the law" (Rom. 13:10 CSB). The law of God is love, and the Bible tells us Jesus is the fulfillment of the law (Matt. 5:17–20). Jesus Christ came in obedience to complete God's love story with His people and set the example for humans in living a holy, sinless life. Such a life cannot be achieved on one's own ability but can be lived through Christ. Love, *agape* love, is the more excellent way.

Our verse today emphasizes the more excellent way for Christians as a process of growth and maturity through faith, hope, and love, with the greatest of these attributes and actions being love. Faith and hope go hand in hand. "Faith is the substance of things hoped for, the evidence of things not seen" (Heb. 11:1 KJV). In other words, faith is the foundation of what a believer stands on in truth and belief, and the evidence of faith is trust and belief in the unseen reality of heaven and eternal life. Faith, hope, and love, and the greatest of these is love. Love is the more excellent way of Christian living, and the fruit of love is faith and hope. Faith exists as recipients of God's love. Hope is a product of God's love growing in faith. The world needs more of the more excellent way of love. The body of Christ needs more love and, in some cases, needs to get back to the more excellent way of love. Faith, hope, and love—God's love is the only way.

> *God has not promised skies always blue,*
> *Flower strewn pathways all our lives through;*
> *God has not promised sun without rain,*
> *Joy without sorrow, peace without pain. . . .*
>
> *But God hath promised strength for the day,*
> *Rest for the labor, light for the way.*
> *Grace for the trials, help from above,*
> *Unfailing sympathy, undying love*
> —Annie Johnson Flint

Let love lead your way today.

THOUGHTS

_____

_____

_____

_____

_____

_____

PRAYER

_____

_____

_____

_____

_____

_____

DAY 83

*"An angel of the Lord spoke to Philip: 'Get up and go south
to the road that goes down from Jerusalem to Gaza'.
(This is the desert road.) So he got up and went."*

Acts 8:26–27 (CSB)

DON'T MISS YOUR SHOT

SEVERAL YEARS AGO while in New York, my wife and I
attended the Broadway musical *Hamilton*, which is about one
of our nation's founding fathers, Alexander Hamilton, and the
establishment of our sovereign nation America. The opening
song stuck in my mind as the cast sang out "you don't need a
legacy, you don't need money, you need peace of mind and don't
miss your shot." The theme of not missing one's shot is expressed
throughout the musical and applies well to the believer to not
miss the shots—opportunities the Lord God puts in our lives to
be part of His best for us.

I recently retired from my place of ministry employment to
move on to a new season of serving the Lord in different capaci-
ties. Surfing is a passion of mine, and I always thought it would be
great to surf on my first day of retirement. When the day came, I
check the conditions. The waves were not great. The weather was
cloudy and cold. There were just a couple of surfers in the water,
and I thought, *I'll go later in the week.* As I got a cup of coffee,
I heard a still small voice say to me, "Don't miss your shot." It
hit me. If someone ever asked me what I did on my first day of
retirement, I would want to be able to reply, "I went surfing."
So I got up and went surfing. It was a blessed time physically,
mentally, and spiritually as it always is. I did not miss my shot.

In our passage today the apostle Philip is given a shot at
ministry glory. Reading through Acts 8, we see he answered the

call and was greatly blessed. On his way to a new ministry field, the Lord gives Philip a divine appointment with an Ethiopian eunuch. As a eunuch the man would have been wealthy and powerful and had great influence over the people in Ethiopia. Yet, he was empty inside. When Philip arrives the eunuch is seeking answers to life that can only be found in God's Word (Acts 8:26–40).

Philip moved out in obedience to God. Obedience is an activity that brings so much good to a believer's life. I heard it once said that sinful actions rob us but obedience enriches us. As we read about Philip's act of obedience, it's easy to recognize that he was spiritually equipped for this opportunity the Lord presented him with. Philip had the answers for the eunuch from the Scriptures he was reading (Isa. 53:7–8). As servants of God, the more we are equipped in readiness, being filled with the Holy Spirit, trusting, and acting in obedience, the more we can step into meeting opportunities the Lord so blesses us with. Being equipped is about knowing God's Word. Paul instructed Timothy to "Be diligent to present yourself to God as one approved, a worker who doesn't need to be ashamed, correctly teaching the word of truth" (2 Tim. 2:15 CSB).

When a servant of God is equipped to engage in the shots of glory for the Lord, amazing fruit will follow. Hebrews 6:10 tells us "For God is not unrighteous to forget your work and labour of love, which ye have shewed toward his name, in that ye have ministered to the saints, and do minister" (KJV). And may I suggest that perhaps the most important aspect in ministry to engage in the shots from God often come when one just shows up—like Philip who "got up and went" not knowing what the journey would entail. Show up and receive what the Lord has in store for you. His blessing is sure to amaze you.

The Ethiopian eunuch was no doubt ministered to by Philip, being baptized in newness of life. It is my belief he went on to share his newness and the gospel. As for Philip, Acts 8 tells us he was physically transcended some twenty miles east of Jerusalem to the town of Azotus where he preached and shared the gospel in all cities on a journey until he came to his final ministry field of Caesarea. Some twenty years later, in Acts 21 Luke tells us that Philip raised a family, four young daughters—virgins who prophesied, which is a testimony of his obedience and faithful influence over his family. Philip did not miss his shot.

So beloved of God, know you are a servant of God and God wants his best for you. Don't miss your shots at the glorious and divine opportunities he provides. Be ready, be an equipped instrument of God. Be obedient and take heed to the leading of the Holy Spirit. Embrace opportunities as a labor of love, and leave the fruit bearing to God.

Don't miss your shot.

THOUGHTS

_____

_____

_____

_____

_____

_____

PRAYER

_____

_____

_____

_____

_____

_____

Devotions
Celebrating
Love & Marriage

DAY 84

"Be willing to serve each other out of respect for Christ."

—Ephesians 5:21 (ERV)

THE PERFECT CIRCLE OF MARRIAGE

THE BIBLE IS clear in that marriage is a God-ordained institution. It is not man-ordained, nor is it a government institution. Marriage is God's institution that reflects the best of God as a crown of His glory. A good and loving marriage is a living testimony of God's purest and truest love displayed for the world to see and to emulate God as the depiction of love that is sacrificial, unconditional, and continual no matter life's circumstances. In other words, a good marriage will be Christlike. It is the two joined together in the flesh as one (Gen. 2:24). Neither is perfect, nor better, nor dominant. Both are imperfect and in need of each other. A godly marriage will be a Christlikeness relationship between husband and wife in harmony with one another and to complement one another.

Our verse for today and the word *serve* speak to an act of humility toward each other in a marriage relationship that fortifies God's love as husband and wife bear one another's burdens for each other as exemplified by Christ (Phil. 2:5–11). The key to serving one another as Christ is the word *willing*. Humility is a choice. It is the choice to die to self and serve others, especially within the marriage relationship. As it was once said: "marriage is not so much finding the right person as it is being the right person." Both husband and wife must choose in faith to serve one another and therefore show respect to Christ and his complete service to mankind.

Paul goes on to instruct wives to serve husbands with the same respect as would be given to Christ (v. 22). The instruction to husbands is to serve their wives with love in the same manner as Christ loved the church—the bride of Christ—and who willingly gave His life for her (v. 25). And husbands, as Christ loves the church as the spiritual head of the church, so too we are to be the spiritual head of the household (vv. 26–30). We see in Paul's letter to the Corinthians that the woman is the glory of man (1 Cor. 11:7). The woman is the spiritual reflection of a man's spiritual leadership, and as such, if there are problems in the marriage, it is most likely a reflection of the husband's own spiritual failures.

In the same respect, godly wives should give the same respect to their godly husband as they give to Christ. And the same love that Christ has for the church (His people) is the same love the husband is to willingly pour out to his wife: sacrificial, unconditional, and unending. The perfect circle for a healthy God-ordained marriage. Men and women are different. They have different desires, different needs, and different emotions. As the wife respects in love, the man is more apt to pour out love for and toward his wife, who then is more apt to lovingly respect her husband, who then pours out more Christlike love to his wife, and on and on goes their expression of love to each other like the endless rings on their fingers. The perfect circle of a godly marriage.

THOUGHTS

_____

_____

_____

_____

_____

_____

PRAYER

_____

_____

_____

_____

_____

_____

DAY 85

"Now faith is the reality of what is hoped for,
the proof of what is not seen . . . . By faith Abraham when
he was called, obeyed . . . . He went out, even though he did not
know where he was going. . . . By faith, even Sarah herself,
when she was unable to conceive offspring . . . considered
that the one who promised [God] was faithful."

—Hebrews 11:1, 8, 11 (CSB)

A MARRIAGE OF FAITH

IN ABRAHAM AND Sarah we find the blessed results of a marriage rooted in faith. It is by faith they obediently left home and family and through many years believed God's promise of a child and many descendants. Their marriage was certainly not perfect nor were they perfect in their faith, but they were willing to obey God and willing to grow in their faith. Paul testifies that Abraham was counted as righteous because of his faith (Rom. 4) and Peter says that Sarah is commended in her faith to allow God to lead her husband Abraham (1 Pet. 3:6).

When the Lord God called me and my wife to sell our house to move from California to the East Coast to plant a church, it was not an easy decision. I found myself wrestling with obeying the call. It did not help that we faced opposition from family and tremendous warfare as we got ready to go, but in the end, it was a blessing unmatched in our sojourn with the Lord. Twelve years later when God called us back to California, we faced much difficulty in making the decision and having to say goodbye to the church body and so many friends and co-workers in the Lord, but we knew that the best life is to be in God's will not our will. As with Abraham, my desire was to fulfill God's call and purpose in service to Him for our lives and to be faithful to His promise and leading. As with Sarah, my wife by faith chose to come alongside me and recognized God's call and purpose for us both in moving back to California. As two are one in marriage and are to cleave to each other in faith, together we cleave to God and His best for us both.

The Bible testifies of Abraham and Sarah's triumphs in faith, and their many failures (Gen. 12, 16, 18, 20), but through it all their marriage was much stronger and prevailed over their individual failures of faith. We eventually see God's promise of a child fulfilled (Gen. 21) on His perfect timing and a nation is birthed and the marriage goes on to enjoy a twenty-year period of tremendous fellowship and faith.

George H. Morrison, a well-known early 1900s preacher from Scotland wrote:

> God does not let us see where we are going. The all-important thing is *the direction*. If moment by moment we are true to him, the land of promise may be left in his hands and God will not force you into acquiescence; there must be faith to answer when he calls. To hear him amid our trials, that is faith; to hear him amid our questions, is faith; to hear his voice in such an age as this is possible; with faith and faith alone.

Faith blesses our lives and marriages, and the practice of faith builds more faith. Abraham and Sarah were a blessed couple because of their faith. They were not perfect, no one is. They dealt with problems and crises rightly and wrongly. They propelled themselves into self-willed failures, follies, and misadventures. They wrestled with God on more than one occasion. They had doubts. They missed the mark at times when asking and seeking for their will in life. Despite such shortcomings, it was their real and sincere faith in God that always brought them back to the right place and right attitude with God. They never failed or came up short when asking and seeking in faith for God's will and purpose in life. Because it is God who is always faithful.

"The steadfast love of the Lord never ceases; His mercies never come to an end; they are new every morning; great is your faithfulness." (Lam. 3:22–23 ESV)

THOUGHTS

_____

_____

_____

_____

_____

_____

_____

PRAYER

_____

_____

_____

_____

_____

_____

_____

DAY 86

"Give my greetings to Priscilla and Aquila, my coworkers in Christ Jesus, who risked their own necks for my life. Not only do I thank them, but so do all the Gentile churches."

—Romans 16:3–4 (CSB)

A SPIRIT-FILLED MARRIAGE

PRISCILLA AND AQUILA are a perfect example of a Spirit-filled marriage. Many scholars suggest that Paul had in mind this couple when instructing on the virtues of a godly marriage in his letter to the Ephesians. No doubt Priscilla and Aquila were a godly couple that lived a life of faith together in coming to know and grow in the love of God and Christ and the ways of a Spirit-filled life.

We read about how Priscilla and Aquila were active in their study and knowledge of Scriptures and the gospel way. They applied the Word and gospel testimony to their lives (Acts 11:26). They were active in ministry and business together, equally yoked in faith and belief (Acts 18). Jesus illustrates the need to stay in relationship with Him saying "I am the vine, you are the branches, he who abides in Me and I in him - will bring forth much fruit; for without me you can do nothing" (John 15:5 NKJV). There is no eternal value without Jesus in your life. This is evident and true in one's personal life as well as married lives. Paul shows the truth of this in his letter to the Corinthians with the beautiful fruit that came forth from Priscilla and Aquila having planted a home church together (1 Cor. 16:19).

In today's verse our Spirit-filled couple were serving with Paul as part of a church plant in Rome and doing so at great risk to their own lives. It takes risk to lead a Spirit-filled life, and it takes risk to lead a Spirit-filled married life reflecting eternal priorities.

Paul is telling the believers in Rome to welcome Priscilla and Aquila as coworkers in Christ. He is not telling them to welcome the couple as successful businesspeople who can give to the church, nor to welcome them as people who will be leaders in the community that can curry favor for the church. Instead, Paul is welcoming them as a married couple who love the Lord and live a Spirit-filled life together and who are willing to lay down their lives at any cost for the cause of Christ. In other words, welcome them as a Spirit-filled blessing to the church.

Later, as Paul writes to Timothy from a Roman prison while awaiting his execution, he urges Timothy to welcome Priscilla and Aquila into the fellowship as they would no doubt be a great blessing to the congregation. They had led the church in Rome for some ten years and had lost everything. Perhaps due to the fires in Rome in AD 67 or because of the persecution against Christians in Rome, they were forced to flee leaving everything behind as Emperor Nero blamed the Christians for the fires. We know that in their service as a married couple in Rome they greatly impacted many upon many lives for Christ. Priscilla and Aquila are always mentioned together in Paul's writings, spotlighting an equally yoked marriage in faith and belief. Serving together with Jesus as the center of the marriage, this Holy Spirit power couple brought forth much fruit in their ministry of love to others. They were blessed to maintain eternal priorities over worldly priorities even when it meant risking it all—which it did.

I thank God for this Spirit-filled marriage and pray my marriage is worthy of such a testimony. I pray that for your marriage as well, beloved in Christ. In Jesus's name.

THOUGHTS

_____

_____

_____

_____

_____

_____

PRAYER

_____

_____

_____

_____

_____

_____

DAY 87

"Beloved, let us love one another: for love is of God;
and everyone that loves is born of God, and knows God."

—1 John 4:7

GOD'S LOVE IN MARRIAGE

GOD IS LOVE, and God is the source of love, and Jesus Christ is the full embodiment of God's love. To know Christ is to know God's love, and to know God's love is to know the selfless, sacrificial, unconditional, agape love of God. As light and heat flow from the sun, so does all love and real love flow from God. God is the mountain from which all rivers of love flow. His love will flow in the deep, tender, closeness, and selflessness of a godly relationship, and His love is paramount to a joyful, fruit bearing, and loving marriage.

God's love is a simple concept. As the children sing: "Jesus loves me, this I know, for the Bible tells me so." The problem becomes when as adults we go looking for love in wrong places and from wrong sources, which can lead to wrong and painful choices. I am reminded of the story of a man who moved to a new town and walked into a restaurant with a full-grown ostrich. Upon the waiter taking the man's order, the ostrich said, "I'll have the same." When it came time to pay the bill the man reached in his pocket and pulled out the exact amount of cash down to the penny including a 20 percent tip. This went on for several days with the ostrich always ordering the same and the man always having the exact amount of cash, including the tip. Finally, the waiter could not resist and asked how the man would always have the exact amount of cash down to the penny in his pocket to pay for the meal. The man told him that a few years ago he was cleaning out his attic and found an old lamp. While rubbing it clean a genie popped out and granted him two wishes. He wished that he would always have the exact amount of change in his pocket for anything he ever bought. Whether he bought a golden chariot or a pack of gum, he would always have the exact amount. The waiter was amazed. "Genius!" He replied. "You'll never lack for anything no matter what it cost." "That's correct" the man said. Then the waiter looked next to the man and asked, "So what's with the ostrich?" The man sighed with embarrassment as he said, "At the time I was lonely and desperately wanted a wife, so my second wish was for a chick with long legs who did everything I did."

Now I know this joke is not completely politically correct, but you get the point. Love is not found in an old lantern. It is not found in people or ostriches. Love, true love, is found in God and is needed for the best marriage a couple can have together. I heard someone once say, "If God's love is not in the roots of a marriage, there will be no fruits of love in the marriage. Love in a marriage begins in the seed in order to produce a tree that brings forth the loving fruits of a good marriage."

God's love in marriage is a call to action. A call to nourish the marriage tree to bring forth good fruit. As Jesus told the disciples: "If I then your Lord and Teacher have washed your feet, you also ought to wash one another's feet" (John 13:14 NKJV). In a marriage these words apply as love in action: sacrifice, surrender, and serving. Being *in* love can be exciting, but it is just a feeling and does not last. Being *of* love creates a unity in marriage that is of depth and choice that is willfully maintained and strengthened by pursuing and being built up by God's love, which both husband and wife can freely ask for and receive. Such love is godly love that lasts forever.

Beloved of God, let the source of love, God, be your guide in finding marriage. Let the perfection of God's love, Jesus Christ, be your example to follow in marriage. Let the Holy Spirit fill your heart in what is always best for your marriage, and let grace be the perfection of God's love in your marriage.

THOUGHTS

_____

_____

_____

_____

_____

_____

PRAYER

_____

_____

_____

_____

_____

_____

Devotions Celebrating the Greatest Gift

DAY 88

*"Today your Savior was born in David's town.
He is the Messiah, the Lord."*

—Luke 2:11 (ERV)

ON ITS SURFACE, the story of Christmas seems completely absurd. A virgin birth, an infant Savior born in a barn. None of it makes sense to any reasonable mind. Which is exactly why the story of Christmas is so perfect.

There is a story of a mighty young king who had fallen hopelessly in love with a beautiful young woman in his kingdom. However, the woman was a commoner of no royalty or elite standing. So how could a mighty king of great royalty pursue this damsel? Should his entourage descend on her cottage with trumpets blaring, gifts aplenty, dazzling her with his royal chariot and fine clothing and massive wealth? Maybe he should just demand her betrothal because of his power and authority? But the problem is if he used his power and wealth to woo the woman to accept his hand in marriage, how would he know for certain if she truly loved him? Instead, the king wisely chose to lay aside his crown and royalty and power and wealth for he knew to gain the woman's love he would have to present himself as her equal, and he wanted marriage to be a choice of the heart for her. So he arrived at her cottage alone, looking like a commoner seeking first the damsel's acceptance and then her love.

Like this story it was Jesus Christ some two thousand-plus years ago who laid down His royalty and power, stepping out of His heavenly kingdom, taking upon Himself all of humanity's weaknesses, becoming a common, helpless Jewish infant. He was born of a virgin, casting doubt on any claims to majesty. He was born in poverty, separating Himself from royalty and alienating Himself from the religious and cultural powers of the day, who in due time tried to block Him from taking His rightful place on the throne. In choosing messengers to spread the news of His right and true standing as the Son of God, Wonderful, Counsellor, the Mighty God, the Everlasting Father, the Prince of Peace, He did not choose sinless majestic angels. No, He chose sinful, imperfect, probably smelly, shepherds to spread the good news.

The whole story strikes of absurdity. Who would think of such a plan? It seems obvious people would mock such a story. What would God think of next, crucifying the King?

And perhaps the most absurd aspect of the story is that God chose humans, imperfect sinful commoners, in every succeeding generation to tell the story of Christmas. The absurdity of it makes it so perfect. Confounding the wise to bless the humble. It is truly a perfect story.

God has written you into His perfect Christmas story. We also have a choice to make. We can claim the story as absurd and like the mockers never accept Christ as our Savior and King. Or, we can be humble like a shepherd, accept His perfect love for us, and go share the good news of the greatest story ever told.

THOUGHTS

_____

_____

_____

_____

_____

_____

PRAYER

_____

_____

_____

_____

_____

_____

DAY 89

"Mary treasured up all these things
and pondered them in her heart."

—Luke 2:19 (NIV)

THE BIRTH OF Christ is the most amazing occurrence in all of history, not only for the miracle of the birth but for the impact this birth had on the world and history. It begins with an eighty-five-mile journey, a five- to six-day trip to the city of Bethlehem for a required census. Joseph walks while Mary rides sidesaddle on a donkey. Swollen and achy from pregnancy and nearing birth, she likely feels every rut and jolt from the weathered and well-traveled dirt road. Arriving in Bethlehem they fade into the mass of travelers also reporting for the census. There is no room at the inn. All booked, no vacancy. It's late. Joseph and Mary are exhausted and desperate as the contractions begin. The innkeeper offers his stable where the animals of the travelers are kept for shelter. The couple does not complain as the contractions grow closer together and more painful. The birth soon begins. No epidermal, no hospital, no sedative to ease the pain. Mary's moans and cries pierce the stable and night air. Joseph, in the role of mid-wife, encourages and comforts Mary. Pushing strenuously with all her strength, the Messiah arrives! Stepping into a trauma-filled world, attached umbilically to a common Jewish girl, the Savior gasps for air and coughs as Mary turns Him over to clear His throat. And then the first cries of the Divine! "For unto us a Child is born" (Isa. 9:6 NKJV). Joseph and a physically exhausted Mary are in awe and wonder, treasuring this moment and all that led up to it. The immaculate conception, the promise of a Savior fulfilled.

Without notice of this royal birth there are no congratulations from heads of states and provinces, only the mice and fleas and grunts and groans from the host of animals who witness this most amazing and glorious of occurrences. Heaven took notice, though. Angels rejoiced, perhaps the captives stirred, a star proudly displayed itself in the night skies marking the birthplace of the Savior of the world.

An announcement went forth to some shepherds in their field who traveled to this place to wonder, worship, and witness this moment and miracle.

Born of a virgin in a barn to a common Jewish girl casts doubts on any claims of majesty. The shepherds, the first evangelists of the gospel age went back to their sheep, telling everyone along the way and glorifying God for all the things they had heard and seen, and those who heard were also astonished (Luke 2:18–20). Joseph mulled over how he could possibly be a father to the Son of God (Luke 2:33). Mary "treasured up all these things that happened." She reflected deeply on the significance of the birth of her child and kept it all in her thoughts. She "pondered them in her heart." She mulled it all over and over, seeking to understand it all while cradling and gazing into the eyes of her baby boy and receiving the call in her heart to mother and nurture her child all the days of his life.

The apostle Paul speaks of the believer's great reward as the crown of righteousness to all those who love and look forward to the promise of our Lord's return (2 Tim. 4:8). I hope your heart is in that place. In the meantime, let us treasure and ponder the first appearing of our Lord as Paul testifies about how Christ defeated death forevermore (2 Tim. 1:10). "O Death where is your sting? O Hades, where is your victory" (1 Cor. 15:55 NKJV).

When was the last time you truly took time and treasured all that brought you to your salvation? When was the last time you pondered what the birth of Christ means to you? Does His peace that surpasses all understanding truly rule your heart today? Let us all make abundant room in our hearts for Jesus this day and all He did for us in defeating death. Treasure, ponder, and embrace Him with open arms and with the grace to be still and know He is God and the Savior of the world.

THOUGHTS

PRAYER

DAY 90

"We love Him, because He first loved us."

—1 John 4:19 (KJV)

EVERY YEAR CHRISTIANS joyfully celebrate the birth of our Savior, Jesus Christ, who on a day some two thousand-plus years ago was born, a Son, a Savior, who redeemed and rules the world. He is called "Wonderful, Counselor, Mighty God, Everlasting Father, Prince of Peace" (Isa. 9:6 NKJV), and I say praise the Lord!

Christmas is the time of year for such a great celebration of what was and what is to come. We celebrate with gifts to one another as a symbol of love, God's love and the greatest gift of love, His son, Jesus Christ. As we rejoice and share gifts at Christmas it is a great time to take stock of our hearts and ask, "Why do I love God?" Certainly, there are a number of reasons to love God. He saved you and delivered you from the bondage of sin. He is kind, merciful, and compassionate. The psalmist David said, "I love the LORD because He heard my voice and my supplications. Because He has inclined His ear to me" (Ps. 116:1–2 NKJV). These are glorious reasons to love God, but let us not forget, as our passage states, the root of all reasons to love God is because He first loved us.

Beloved, you may not feel loved by God today because of personal circumstances, or a rejecting heart, but that does not negate God's love for you. You see God's love is perfect. It is not dependent on you or your actions but only on God. The Bible says His love is complete in that on the day of judgment you shall be confident in His love because His perfect love drives out fear and doubt. To know God loves you is to know true grace from a place of kindness, compassion, and tenderness that is not found in the world but only in the love of God. And to know that love is to love one another in truth and sincerity of heart. Because He first loved you, He sent His son to die for you. To reset the broken bones of sin and to restore your heart back into a love relationship with Him.

Beloved of God, do not fear or doubt God's love for you. If you do, your heart will grow hard and bitter. Rather, embrace the love He has for you, and your heart will be filled with such a love for Him you won't be able to stop yourself from sharing that love with others. Your love for God will overflow and pour out of you. For unto you a Son is given, and you love Him because He first loved you. Merry Christmas!

THOUGHTS

_____

_____

_____

_____

_____

_____

PRAYER

_____

_____

_____

_____

_____

_____

DAY 91

*"For the wages of sin is death; but the gift of God
is eternal life in Christ Jesus our Lord."*

—Romans 6:23 (KJV)

SUCH IS THE greatest gift ever! For unto us the child was born, the son was given to save the human race. The Bible tells us Jesus Christ is the Son of David. He is God's sovereign King. Appointed, rejected, but a King who will return. Jesus is also the Son of Mary—God's supernatural child from a virgin, a divine birth of divine truth. The Bible tells us Jesus is the Son of Man— the servant child who suffered physically, submitting to the Father's will, establishing the blueprint for love and obedience to God. Jesus is also described as the Son of God, the Savior child. The only acceptable sacrifice that takes the wages of sin away forever. The only Savior who can lead us to eternal heaven. And the child, this Son will return to rule the world in His righteousness and justice to bring real peace on earth. "For He must reign till He has put all enemies under His feet. The last enemy that will be destroyed is death (1 Cor. 15:25–26 NKJV).

To the woman at the well, Jesus speaking of Himself said, "if you know the gift of God and who it is who says to you, 'Give Me a drink,' you would have asked Him, and He would have given you living water (John 4:10 NKJV). The apostle Paul proclaims, "Thanks be unto God for His unspeakable gift (2 Cor. 9:15 KJV). Jesus Christ, born of peasant virgin in a tiny obscure village, lived in humility, suffered rejection, and then was handed over to His enemies. He was mocked and tried, beaten beyond recognition, nailed to a cross between two thieves, laid to rest in a borrowed tomb, yet rose again. He was loved and hated, but there has never been one who impacted the world so greatly. It has been said that of all the military forces that ever rolled across land or powered across seas, nor all the kings that ever reigned nor all the govern- ments that ever existed put together have not impacted life on earth so overwhelmingly and powerfully as has the one single life of the humble carpenter, Jesus Christ.

Jesus is the greatest gift to this world. The gift of God for eternal life. Not only as the child who came to show us the way of life and life everlasting, but also as the man who died to complete the way, so He can return as conquering King.

THOUGHTS

PRAYER

DAY 92

"Thanks be unto God for His unspeakable gift."

—2 Corinthians 9:15 (NKJV)

THE APOSTLE PAUL exhorted the church in Corinth on the foundational principles of giving and why as God's people we are to give of what God has provided for us. Paul speaks of the blessings and benefits that go along with giving, and then when he tries to describe God's gift of Jesus Christ to us the only word Paul can come up with is *unspeakable*.

Paul's description shows that our minds are limited in their ability to grasp the fullness and glory of God's gift Jesus Christ. It is too great, too glorious, to adequately describe and yet as believers we know it is the greatest of gifts. All throughout the Bible, from Genesis to Revelation, from creation to the fall, from the call of Abraham through the times of Judges, from the prophets to Christ, to the Apostolic age, and on to the Apocalypse and the consummation of the age, no word, no language, no expression, no description can do justice to the incomparable message of love, salvation, hope and redemption all contained in the unspeakable gift, Jesus Christ. It is the gift of unspeakable love—unconditional, universal, and unmerited. Yet, even in our sinful states, God commanded His love to us anyway and gave His son to die for us (Rom. 5:8).

Jesus Christ is the gift of unspeakable greatness and glory. He walks with God (John 1:1-2), He is God (Titus 2:13). He is head over all things (Eph. 1:22). He is all-knowing and life-giving (John 1:4). Being given a gift of such greatness and glory can only lead one's heart to thanks. We have been given the gift of Jesus Christ and all His benefits and blessings of love, hope, peace, comfort, and joy in life. Being given such greatness and glory unspeakable and divine my own heart cries out THANKS BE TO GOD FOR HIS UNSPEAKABLE GIFT!

One night as people came across the nativity scene in a church yard, there was a dog lying next to the baby Jesus. It was a stray dog looking for a place of comfort and peace and protection to rest its weary head. The dog was wise to draw near to Jesus for such a place. This Christmas, draw near to Him, and He will draw near to you. Draw near with a true heart in full assurance of faith, having your heart sprinkled from an evil conscience, and your body washed with pure water.

Merry Christmas and thanks be to God for His unspeakable gift.

THOUGHTS

_____

_____

_____

_____

_____

_____

PRAYER

_____

_____

_____

_____

_____

_____

DAY 93

"Peace I leave with you, My peace I give to you."

—John 14:27 (NKJV)

PAUL TELLS US of God's unspeakable gift—His son Jesus Christ (2 Cor. 9:15). So great a gift, so complete, so glorious, so overwhelming it is unspeakable in human terms. It is a gift unmatched in love, mercy, salvation, hope, and redemption, one that keeps on giving.

From our verse today, we see that Jesus Christ, the unspeakable gift, is the one and only one who can give us unspeakable peace. Jesus doesn't give us a peace the world can provide, a peace between nations, people, or cultures, but rather He gives us a peace between a person and their Creator. A peace that ends the separation and alienation of a person with God. A peace that surpasses all understanding (Phil. 4:7). A peace with God that leads to a life of peace in God all one's days. He gives a peace that overcomes us not only in the blessings of life but also in the hardships of life. In the world there will always be trials and tribulations, but in Christ we have peace because Jesus overcame the world (John 16:33). After his dear friend James was martyred and seeing how pleased the religious leaders were over this execution, King Herod threw Peter in jail. Chained between two soldiers, Peter slept like a baby even though it was the night before he was to be executed (Acts 12:6).

The prophet Jeremiah shared God's heart when he said: "for I know the thoughts that I think toward you, saith the Lord, thoughts of peace, and not of evil, to give you an expected end" (Jer. 29:11 KJV)—the hope of ultimate peace in heaven. The prophet Isaiah tells us God "will keep him in perfect peace, Whose mind is stayed on [God], because he trusts in [God]" (Isa. 26:3 NKJV).

As the shepherds looked down on baby Jesus lying in a manger in a stable, their wonder and joy was due to the gift of a Messiah, the one who has conquered the world in defeating sin and death. In Jesus they saw a warrior for the kingdom of God, a King who would subdue nations and every enemy of God in complete and final victory. Knowing this victory, we have unspeakable peace in Jesus Christ. All our troubles and fears from the world can be cast out of our hearts, leaving His peace to reign.

The heart is where peace begins, beloved. Jesus says: "let not your hearts be troubled. Believe in God; believe also in me" (John 14:1 ESV). Believe today in Jesus Christ! Receive Him as your Lord and Savior, and let unspeakable peace fill your heart and life.

THOUGHTS

PRAYER

DAY 94

"Praise God in heaven, and on earth let there be peace to the people who please Him."

—Luke 2:14 (ERV)

THE CHRISTMAS STORY is an amazing testimony of the love God has for you, not in just the gift of eternal life through His son Jesus Christ, but also for the peace that surpasses all understanding that comes with your perfect gift from heaven. And yet, on its surface the story of makes no sense to reasonable minds. To think a story of a virgin birth, a baby as a savior; angels and hosts worshipping a child is true, which is exactly why the story of Christmas is so perfect.

The Lord God Almighty, the King of kings, the Lord of lords, stepped out of heaven, leaving His royal throne and place to take on all of humanity's weaknesses, failures, and sin. A commoner bearing no claims to royalty, alienated Himself from the powers that be who would also block Him from taking His rightful place on the throne. Then God chose imperfect human messengers to spread the good news of His perfect gift of love and salvation. He could have chosen angels to do His bidding, but rather God began the pronouncement of the Savior by using defective, smelly, shepherds from the fields to spread the news that would be carried to every generation. It stinks of absurdity. Who would concoct such a crazy plan? The people will mock such a story: "what will God come up with next? Crucifying His Son?

"What manner of child shall this be?" A perfect child, a perfect man. The story of Christmas is so perfect it confounds the wise and gives blessing and understanding to the humble, even the common folk. And what manner of love God has bestowed on us that we should be called sons of God (John 1:12, Rom. 8:14). So what manner of person ought you to be in your relationships and conversations? What manner of godliness are you as a partaker of this absurd but gloriously true story?

Beloved of God, know and acknowledge that God has written you into His Christmas story. It may be crazy and absurd in the natural sense, but it is perfect in the eternal sense. Turn to Jesus if you haven't already. Turn to the perfect one. Call on Him. Accept His invitation to love and salvation and then go live for Him and Him alone.

Merry Christmas!

THOUGHTS

PRAYER

DAY 95

*"Behold, a virgin shall be with child, and shall bring forth
a son, and they shall call his name Emmanuel.
Which being interpreted is, God with us."*

—Matthew 1:23 (KJV)

EMMANUEL, GOD WITH us. God stepping out of heaven as
His Son, Jesus Christ, who came in the flesh. But why in the form
of a baby, a child?

God is the Creator of heaven and earth, of you and me,
and God desires and wants a relationship with each of us on a
personal level. He desires for us to engage in His creation as it
is a gift and blessing for us. He desires for us to have a personal
relationship with Him on an intimate and loving level that goes
both ways. "Now there was leaning on Jesus' bosom one of His
disciples, whom Jesus loved" (John 13:23 NKJV). I believe in
establishing a reciprocal, intimate, loving, and caring relationship with God, who showed us just how much he wants and
needs us in such a relationship by sending His Son first as a baby,
a child. It is Christ as a baby and child that evokes compassion
in all of us. It is the love and compassion of a parent and child.
When Pharoah's daughter found the baby Moses in a basket by
the river, the Bible tells us when she opened the basket "she saw
the child, and behold, the babe wept. So she had compassion on
him" (Exod. 2:6 NKJV). Compassion evokes joy and the natural
desire to be in an intimate relationship. Elizabeth, upon hearing
news of Mary's pregnancy, rejoiced, and the babe in the womb
even leaped with joy (Luke 1:44).

What are some of the benefits and blessings of an intimate
loving relationship with the almighty God? For starters He
promises to always be with us (Gen. 28:15, Heb. 13:5). The Bible
tells us the Lord God is our rest (Exod. 33:14, Matt. 11:28–30).

God promises to be our strength in the battles (Duet. 20:1, Matt. 12:20, Rom. 8:37–39). He promises to be our comfort (Isa. 43:2, 2 Cor. 1:3–4). God is our friend (James 2:23, John 15:15), and He promises to be with us to the end (Matt. 28:19–20). And these are just some of the wonderful promises of blessings and benefits we have with an intimate relationship with God.

Christmas is the celebration of God's perfect gift to us, a gift of love and salvation and invitation to a relationship with the real and living God. Jesus Christ, the gift, is the only baby with such promise and qualities. He was and is the only baby to be called "Wonderful, Counselor, Mighty God, Everlasting Father, Prince of Peace (Isa. 9:6 NKJV). So revere and celebrate the baby Jesus, the child God who came to invite you into a personal relationship with a personal God.

Merry Christmas!

THOUGHTS

_____

_____

_____

_____

_____

_____

PRAYER

_____

_____

_____

_____

_____

_____

Devotions Celebrating the Victory

DAY 96

"Then, behold, the veil of the temple was torn in two
from top to bottom."

—Matthew 27:51 (NKJV)

EASTER TO THE Christian is the most important celebration
as it commemorates the victory we have over death because and
through the resurrected Christ. The apostle Paul says in his letter
to the Romans: "For if we have been united together in the likeness of His death, certainly we also shall be in the likeness of
His resurrection" (Rom. 6:5 NKJV). The apostle Peter wrote that
"Because of His great mercy he has given us a new birth into
a living hope through the resurrection of Jesus Christ from the
dead" (1 Pet. 1:3 CSB).

Through Jesus Christ, the believer is given direct access to
God. The veil being torn in two is the great symbol of that access,
and it also tells the world that the old, religious way to access
God had to be shredded. What a moment in time this event was!
The temple priest wondered how Christ followers would respond
to the crucifixion. There was an inexplicable darkness over the
land for three hours, and we are told the moment Jesus gave up
His spirit, suddenly the veil some eighty feet high and six inches
thick was torn in two from top to bottom. A supernatural occurrence, no doubt the priests were watching in terror. The religious
leaders should have been drawing people to God to access the
fullness of His truth and glory. Instead, they turned Judaism
into a religion of corruption, where its leaders became as the
Nicolaitans lording over rather than leading the people.

The Bible speaks of the mystery of God's glory being hidden
by religion and the veil being a symbol of that hidden truth and
hidden access to God. In the book of Exodus, after being in the
presence of God, Moses veiled his face as God's glory faded,

symbolizing a reflection of man's heart and man's religion hiding the deeper truths and mysteries of God. We know why the chicken crossed the road—to get to the other side. The mystery remains why did the chicken *want* to get to the other side? There must have been something it needed.

Paul speaks of the old way of religion as the ministry of condemnation which had glory, but the new way in Christ as the ministry of righteousness, which has much greater glory (2 Cor. 3:9–16). For if what passed away was glorious, what remains is much more glorious: the believers' positional salvation in Christ. Moses had to put a veil over his face so that the children of Israel would not see the fading glory, because their minds were blinded. The veil symbolically remains today as the Old Testament still hides the true meaning and glory of God to those who don't believe. Only in Christ, who tore the veil in two, can the veil of the old and hidden way be removed to unlock the fullness and mysteries of God when one gives their life to Jesus. Mark tells us the glorious mysteries of God are revealed to us (Mark 4:11). Revelation speaks to the truth of the gospel message, hidden for ages, being revealed in Christ Jesus (Rev. 10:7), and when that message is read, the believer can understand the secret truth of God in Christ (Eph. 3:4).

Sadly, there are veils of religion today keeping people from resurrection victory in Christ Jesus—not only through false religions, but through false doctrines and false movements in the church: Prosperity, name it and claim it, kingdom now, winds of doctrine that come and go tossing innocent hearts to and fro in their relationship with God. The veils of one world ecumenical movements, religions of politics and policies. The personal veils of sin and idolatry. All these things blind and hide the truths of God and His glory, truths we need in this world and in our personal lives. Are there veils in your life today that need shredding to lead you into a deeper faith with God?

The resurrection victory is a stark reminder of the shredding of religion as the temple veil was torn in two, the shredding of man's hinderances to access the fullness of God. Where religion blinds and binds, Jesus Christ sets one free to see, hear, speak, and shout if needed about the wonderous glories of God, which are no longer a mystery but are accessible to all who trust and believe in Jesus Christ as their Lord and Savior. "Ask and it will be given to you; seek, and you will find; knock, and the door will be opened to you." (Matt. 7:7 NKJV).

THOUGHTS

PRAYER

DAY 97

"Then Simon Peter came, following him (John), and went
into the tomb; and he saw the linen clothes lying there."

—John 20:6 (NKJV)

THE EMPTY TOMB and blood-stained linen graveclothes of
death that remained as our Lord walked out of the grave into His
resurrection gives the believer unmistakable and unfailing hope,
and undisputed victory over death and the grave through the
resurrected Jesus Christ. Glory! "O death, where is your sting? O
grave, where is your victory?" (1 Cor. 15:55 KJV).

As you and I gaze through our hearts into the empty tomb
on Easter Sunday, rejoice in the resurrection victory we have in
Jesus Christ. As we see the linen clothes, it is a reminder how
as believers, born again in Christ, we are required to put off
our old selves, the old graveclothes, and put on the new clothes
of righteousness we have in Christ (Eph. 4:22–24). Put on the
new transformed you and take off the old grave clothes we were
walking around in that testified of a destiny of eternal death.

The apostle John wrote of the power of Christ's resurrection
in the resurrection of Lazarus. Four days dead that by the time
Jesus and the disciples arrived, it is perceived nothing could
be done. Even Martha admitted his decaying body "stinketh"
by then. But Jesus merely spoke, and Lazarus came forth. John
wrote that Jesus said, "loose him and let him go" (John 11:44
NKJV). Take off the stinky linen strips that bind him and the
graveclothes and let him go put on fresh new clothing. Put off the
old, and put on the new.

The Bible says that the "wages of sin is death" (Rom. 6:23
NKJV), and "all have sinned and fall short of the glory of God"
(Rom. 3:23 NKJV). So it goes that without Christ, without being
born again and clothed in His righteousness, one is just a dead

person walking around in their graveclothes of eternal death. However, the good news is that as new creations in Christ, we no longer live in sin's corruption and death over our lives, but rather we are transformed vessels through the Spirit of God. Too many Christians today choose to not shed their graveclothes and put on their new clothes of righteousness. They remain beaten and condemned by the law. They are bound by the tomb of their mind rather than being set free to walk in the power and resurrection of Jesus Christ. Saved but not submitted to obedience, they are set apart but not surrendered.

Paul gives the believer the promise that as we are united in the likeness of our Lord's death, we will also be in the likeness of His resurrection (Rom. 6:5). When the Lord comes again it will be with the righteousness of God accompanied by His army from heaven on white horses, clothed in fine linen, pure white and clean (Rev. 19:14). Until that day, walk in the promised righteousness you are clothed in through Jesus Christ. Step out of the tomb of death, lay down the graveclothes of sin, and testify to the world of the power of the resurrection through the changed you.

THOUGHTS

PRAYER

DAY 98

*"Dear friends, I wanted very much to write to you
about the salvation we all share together. But I felt the need
to write to you about something else: I want to encourage
you to fight hard for the faith that God gave His holy people.
God gave this faith once, and it is good for all time."*

—Jude 1:3 (ERV)

AS WE REFLECT this month on Easter and Christ's triumph
over death through His resurrection, which grants and guaran-
tees eternal life to all who believe in Him, may we also recognize the call to fight for this victory we have. It was our Lord
who delivered us from our sins and with us His gospel truth.
He defeated death by paying the ultimate price for our sins to
be forgiven. It is His fight that has become his followers fight
today. The apostle Paul admonished Timothy saying, "Fight the
good fight of the faith. Take hold of eternal life to which you were
called and about which you have made a good confession in the
presence of many witnesses" (1 Tim. 6:12 CSB).

In our passage today, Jude is compelled to address the
churches of Asia Minor about the apostates and false teachers
that were corrupting the churches from within and steering
hearts of the faithful astray from the true redemptive work of the
gospel of Jesus Christ. Rather than writing about the faith, Jude
delivers a stern warning to the churches. He says it was needed
to address the heresies. The King James Version states it was
"needful," indicating that Jude wrestled with this matter and was
greatly distressed in his heart to warn the churches. The Holy
Spirit had been impressing upon and convicting Jude to write
about this attack on the faith.

How many countless hours have you, the believer in Christ,
been kept up at night, contemplating needful spiritual matters

that you must attend to? As followers of Christ, we've all been there and have glorious testimonies from such times. It is evidence of our own fight for the faith. The hardening and fortifying of our faith and spiritual walks with the Lord.

Our passage is a moment in time in Jude's fight for the faith. He encourages the reader to "fight hard" or "earnestly contend" (as the KJV puts it) for the faith. It is a severe fight, leading to exhaustion. In other words, our fight for the faith is continuous as we journey through life until our Lord receives us. We contend and fight for the gospel of Jesus Christ, the good news of Christ as Savior, the way of redemption and salvation through the life, death, and victorious resurrection of Jesus Christ. This is the believer's fight. This is what we are to earnestly contend for in our lives.

The believer's fight for faith is on a corporate level (the church as the body of Christ) and on a personal level. Peering over the landscape of Christianity today we see so much of it littered with heresy and corruption. prosperity and healing, happiness and joy, becoming like gospel rather than sacrifice and suffering for the gospel of faith. Misguided faith where destination matters little, but treasures along the journey here on earth mean everything. But Jude reminds us all to fight hard, earnestly contend for the true faith you have received. The true gospel of Jesus Christ, in whom Him alone is our victory.

THOUGHTS

_____

_____

_____

_____

_____

_____

PRAYER

_____

_____

_____

_____

_____

_____

_____

DAY 99

"But the man said, 'Don't be afraid. You are looking for Jesus from Nazareth, the one who was killed on the cross. He has risen from death! He is not here. Look, here is the place they put him when he was dead. Now go and tell his followers.'"

—Mark 16:6-- (ERV)

HE IS RISEN! Go and tell His followers. As we look at the risen Christ, the victory we have in the empty grave, are you sharing such glorious news to those who believe, and those who don't? Are we living in and living out our joy of victory for all to see? I read somewhere of the believer's life being equated to punctuation marks. For some, the resurrection is like a comma whereby they pause to listen, reflect about Easter for a moment or day or two, and that's it. Back to the hustle and bustle of life. For others, the resurrection victory is like a halting period. It's a downer of an empty ritual whereby one does not partake in the victory celebration, but rather as an outsider looking in.

For the disciples of the Lord, the death of Christ was probably like a big bold period. No victory celebration. Their Messiah was dead and buried. Hopes and expectations were crushed and rotting away in a tomb. But then came news that the tomb was empty. Their hearts moved from a period to a question mark. What happened? The grave is empty? Where is our Lord? Then the disciples remember! Gone is the halting period. The question marks have been removed. The only punctuation mark exuding from their hearts was a big, bold exclamation mark! He is risen! An exclamation of gratitude and praise for the resurrection of Jesus Christ and the hope of salvation in Him. Victory over death!

The resurrection victory exclaims the power of a transformed life believers have in Christ. It is the power of a life full of joy and hope. It is the power that transformed Peter's fear into courage.

James's doubt was transformed into faith. Saul the pharisee was transformed into Paul the apostle, turning from persecution to preaching. Beloved of Christ, the victory you have in the resurrected Christ transformed your life into a big, bold exclamation point for Jesus. Victory is to be on our hearts and on display every day. He is risen! There are no contenders to defeat Jesus nor the believer. We are to be seen by others in the world as an exclamation point for the Lord, living in and for the victory we have already received. Go tell other followers with joy and encouragement and exhortations of our victory! Share the good news of an expected end to each other and all people God sends into our lives.

THOUGHTS

_____

_____

_____

_____

_____

_____

PRAYER

_____

_____

_____

_____

_____

_____

*"For I am commanding you today to love the Lord your God,
to walk in His ways, and to keep his commands,
statutes, and ordinances, so that you may live and multiply,
and the Lord your God may bless you in the land
you are entering to possess."*

Deuteronomy 30:16 (CSB)

*When these things begin to happen, look up and lift up your
heads, because your redemption draws near*

Luke 21:28 (NKJV)

With His Grace & Love,

Pastor David Massie

Scripture Index

About the Author

AS A DEDICATED follower of Christ, David Massie brings a unique voice to his devotionals. Being a pastor, Bible teacher, biblical counselor, church planter, as well as a businessman and entrepreneur, he shares real-life experiences through Scripture from a world that is often in rebellion to biblical values.

Born in Minneapolis, Minnesota, David moved with his family to California at the age of twelve. In college he earned a Bachelor of Arts in public policy and a Master of Arts in urban and regional planning, using them as a platform to launch a real estate career. He is still active in real estate today as an investor and owner of a property management company. David has been blessed to be married to his wife for over thirty-eight years. Their wonderful son is the apple of their eyes and is joined by the most wonderful of daughters-in-law. David and his wife live in Southern California with their beloved golden retrievers, Anna and Elianna.

Having given his life to the Lord in 1994, David has a passion for sharing God's word in a loving, compassionate, and thought-provoking way that blesses and challenges people. He understands the importance of serving others with Christ's love and that serving is the way one stays strong in faith. David believes serving can bring hardships of its own, but it also keeps one busy in the blessings of a life of faith. It is in our service to God we emulate our Lord Jesus to the glory of God, and that the abundant life is to love God and serve others through God's love. All goodness and love of God is represented in His son Jesus Christ who willingly died for all sin thus pardoning all who believe from the sentence of eternal death in sin and that cherishing such an act of divine love, one walks in and can fulfill the love of God in their own life.

One of David's favorite Scriptures is "But when these things begin to take place, stand up and lift your heads, because your redemption is near" (Luke 21:28 CSB). Jesus is speaking to the signs of the end times and His return. The eternal age for believers. David takes to heart this Scripture for believers not to be focused on the "when" of our Lord's return, but rather focus on a readiness that the Lord can return at any moment. So live with a look-up attitude every day in anticipation of His return. Be doing everything as to the glory of the God (1 Cor. 10:31) as life is not about us, but about helping others get to know the love of Jesus. Pastor David loves to close his sermons exhorting the flock to "remember to always LOOK UP!"